Enchantments

OF THE *Mississippi*

Enchantments

OF THE Mississippi

a CONTEMPLATIVE JOURNEY
of TIME AND PLACE

THOMAS BECKNELL

illustrations by KARI VICK

— BEAVER'S POND PRESS —
Saint Paul, Minnesota

Edited by Sara Ensey
Illustrated by Kari Vick
Production editor: Alicia Ester
Cover illustration by: Thomas Becknell

ISBN 13: 978-1-64343-760-6
Library of Congress Catalog Number: 2021920902
Printed in the United States of America
First Printing: 2022
26 25 24 23 22   5 4 3 2 1

Book design and typesetting by Athena Currier

Beaver's Pond Press
939 Seventh Street West
Saint Paul, MN 55102
(952) 829-8818
www.BeaversPondPress.com

Contact Thomas Becknell at thomasbecknell.com for speaking engagements, book club discussions, and interviews.

for PJ and for Jim

PRAISE FOR
Enchantments of the Mississippi

Thomas Becknell invites us to join him as he sets out to find some spiritual connections and a sense of the sacred along the banks of the Upper Mississippi River. His search leads him from his own Twin Cities home to select points south, and to such towns as Prescott, Grafton, Nauvoo, and Hannibal. This exploration is about both geography and humanity. Through his own travels and readings, Thomas—and we—learn more about the circumstances that have led various people to gather along the banks of the Great River, over the years. By the conclusion of this memoir, we may all agree with something American author and naturalist Henry David Thoreau once wrote: "What a piece of wonder a river is." *He* had traveled along this part of the Mississippi, too.

—Corinne H. Smith, author of *Westward I Go Free: Tracing Thoreau's Last Journey*

In his exploration of "the terrible and wonderful river that is the Mississippi," Thomas Becknell draws on personal experience, local river lore and history, and beautifully integrated research provided by various river guardians and guides. Becknell's writing is precise and lyrical. This is a book to savor.

—Lisa Knopp, author of *What the River Carries: Encounters with the Mississippi, Missouri, and Platte*

Thomas Becknell draws on deeply reflective personal experience and wide reading in the literature and histories of the Mississippi River to create this wonderfully evocative book. This lyrical account highlights the complexities and paradoxes of America's greatest river. What a great, distinctive read!

—Patrick Nunnally, founding editor of *Open Rivers: Rethinking Water, Place, and Community*, and lecturer, University of Minnesota

This change in the weather was favorable to our contemplative mood, and disposed us to dream yet deeper at our oars, while we floated in imagination farther down the stream of time.

—HENRY DAVID THOREAU

The Mississippi, sister of the Ganges,
Main artery of earth in the western world,
Is waiting to become
In the spirit of America, a sacred river.

—JEAN TOOMER

CONTENTS

ACKNOWLEDGMENTS

I AM DEEPLY GRATEFUL FOR ALL WHO INSPIRED AND CHEERED ME on throughout this journey, especially—

- Pamela Erwin, who joined me midway as my wife and dearest companion
- Don Postema, who encouraged my setting out and kept me going
- John Becknell, my beloved brother
- Paul Bogard, Wayne Roosa, Gabrielle Lawrence, Diana Magnuson
- Dave Krahn and Roger Hardy
- The Reverend Jim Bear Jacobs, Healing Minnesota Stories
- Cole Williams, poet and author of *Hear the River Dammed*
- The staff of the Gale Family Library, Minnesota Historical Society
- The many docents, volunteers, and guides along the Mississippi River

Special thanks to Kari Vick for her superb, contemplative drawings of the river's enchantments.

And to my publisher and the brilliant editors, designers, and staff of Beaver's Pond Press—

- Lily Coyle, Alicia Ester, Athena Currier, Sara Ensey, Becca Hart, Taylor Blumer

Thanks, also, to these nearby guardians of the Mississippi River—

- Joe Barten, Lower Mississippi River Water Management Organization
- Minnesota Water Stewards and Freshwater
- Metropolitan Council Environmental Services, especially Dave Gardner
- Friends of the Mississippi River
- Friends of Pool 2

Grateful acknowledgment is made for permission to reprint the following:

Excerpt from "Brown River, Smile" by Jean Toomer. First published in *Pagany, a Native Quarterly* 3, no. 1 (Winter 1932); collected in *The Uncollected Works of American Author Jean Toomer, 1894–1967*, Edwin Mellen Press, Lewiston, NY, 2003. Reprinted by permission of Edwin Mellen Press.

Excerpt from "The River" by Ruth F. Brin, in *Harvest: Collected Poems and Prayers*, Holy Cow! Press, Duluth, MN, 1999. Reprinted by permission of Holy Cow! Press.

Excerpt from "The Confluence" by Peter Neil Carroll, in *Riverborne: A Mississippi Requiem*, Higganum Hill Books, Higganum, CT, 2008. Reprinted by permission of Peter N. Carroll.

Excerpt from "Bluffing" by Dick Stahl. Published by *Big River Magazine*, 2016. Reprinted by permission of the late Dick Stahl.

Excerpt from "Flashback" by Angela Shannon, in *Singing the Bones Together*, Tia Chucha Press, 2003. Reprinted by permission of Angela Shannon.

PROLOGUE

Consider the River

Who can know the river, the unknown river?
Buoys and charts are words on the river of the mind,
And a poem is a crystal, ice from the river,
Formed when the yearning of the heart is defined.

—"The River" by Ruth F. Brin

I N THE ROCKY REGION OF MINNESOTA'S NORTH COUNTRY, waters that will become the Mississippi seep from a shallow lake surrounded by other lakes and ponds, bogs, and majestic stands of red and white pine. The stream meanders for miles through fields, fumbles to find its way, then gathers speed as it draws to itself the waters of creeks and streams and is itself drawn on toward the southeast. When it gets to the city of Minneapolis, the river pours over the Saint Anthony Falls dam and slips through a gorge to merge with the Minnesota River, moving on into an enchanted land of bluffs and palisades known as the Driftless Area.

For the Dakota, De Wakpa Taŋka, this was the great river.

One clear evening, late in the summer of 2020, I found myself in Minneapolis on the Stone Arch Bridge, watching the great river pour across the upper Saint Anthony Falls dam. Long before the dam was built, these falls were sacred to the Dakota and the Ojibwe. The Dakota knew them as Owamniyomni, and the Ojibwe called them Kababikah, or Kichi-Kababikah. Above the falls, beyond the Third Avenue Bridge, rise the solid, twin towers of the Hennepin Avenue Bridge. Downstream, below the lower falls, azure-blue lights trace the gentle arches of the new Saint Anthony Falls Bridge. The old steel truss bridge it replaced collapsed under rush-hour traffic and fell into the river on the

first August evening of 2007. Thirteen were killed and many
more injured.

Between the Hennepin Avenue Bridge and the Saint Anthony
Falls Bridge is this beautiful, curving Stone Arch Bridge, built
by the railroad baron James J. Hill. Now serving as a pedestrian bridge, it connects the Father Hennepin Bluffs on the east
bank with the old mill ruins of Minneapolis on the west bank.
On any ordinary summer evening, you might see a horse-drawn
carriage moving slowly past a sidewalk café on Saint Anthony's
cobblestoned main street. On the other side of the river, you
might spot Guthrie theatergoers standing high above the river
on a projecting ledge, drinks in hand, gazing out upon the Minneapolis riverfront. Glowing letters, spelling out the name of the
current play, would be rising up the vertical marquee like embers
up a flue.

But the summer of 2020 was anything but ordinary. The
sidewalk café was closed and the Guthrie marquee was dark.
Pedestrians passed me, wearing masks; many struggled just to
breathe. Our social structures have been strained, close to the
point of rupture. A tenacious pandemic, the violence of systemic
racial injustice, and a climate in crisis have shattered our illusions, exposing the stark realities of what we have become. That
summer, some idols were pulled down, and some icons slipped
away—the prophetic voice of John Lewis, and the judicial voice
of Ruth Bader Ginsburg fell silent.

I've come to the river for solace. It's brought consolation in
years past, and I want to reconnect with its mystical spirit. I stood
on this bridge—as I have so often stood on Mississippi River
bridges—and I thought about John Lewis, walking a bridge in
1965 across the Alabama River, and of his long life of influence.

Around here, the names of Saint Anthony and Father Hennepin are ubiquitous and have been working on me like an incantation. Saint Anthony never saw the falls that bear his name; and the falls Father Hennepin named are now no more than a dam. Anthony and Hennepin were Franciscans, separated in time by as many centuries as I am from Father Hennepin. To be a Franciscan, then as now, is to follow the rule of Saint Francis, living "as pilgrims and strangers in this world, serving the Lord in poverty and humility."

Father Louis Hennepin served by exploring. Sent by Louis XIV to accompany La Salle as a missionary, Hennepin was in turn sent by La Salle to search the upper Mississippi River and was caught by a band of Mdewakanton Dakota, who brought him to the falls in the spring of 1680. Hennepin promptly named the falls for his hero, Saint Anthony of Padua, a Portuguese holy man and friend of the famed Saint Francis of Assisi. In the Middle Ages, Saint Anthony had been known for his preaching. According to one medieval legend, Saint Anthony once preached to the fishes in the seaside town of Rimini when no one else would listen. Today, those who have lost things, or have lost themselves, might invoke Saint Anthony's assistance. While Hennepin never became a saint, he wrote a book in 1683, *Description de la Louisiane*, which sold well in Paris and provided the first written description of the falls.

These falls gained nothing from their European christening but the attention that would prove to be their damming. The Dakota and Ojibwe had met and traded at these falls for many generations. And for a while, the Europeans, too, responded to the magic of the falls. Travelers came from far away to gaze at them in wonder. But in time, commercial and industrial interests desecrated them. By 1838, both the Dakota and Ojibwe nations had ceded their surrounding lands, and within another generation, Spirit Island—just below the falls—had vanished.

Today, to imagine the original splendor of the falls, you might need to visit a corner of the third floor in the nearby Minneapolis Institute of Art and ponder the little paintings of Seth Eastman and Henry Lewis. Their visions, framed in 1848 were, even then, redolent with nostalgia. And by the time George Catlin painted his broad blue vision of the falls in 1871, and Albert Bierstadt his warm, golden canvas a few years later, the Falls of Saint Anthony had long receded into romantic legend.

Up and down the Mississippi River, pilgrims seek the hallowed edges—the shrines and sites revered and holy. On both the eastern banks and western banks are sites made sacred by death, by burial, by time, topography, and worship. People sometimes feel the call of these sacred places and go on pilgrimages.

Pilgrims come to where the river flows through Memphis, where Martin Luther King Jr. was martyred, to renew themselves and carry on his dream. They come to the crossroads of Highways 61 and 49 in Clarksdale, Mississippi, the river town where Robert Johnson made his pact with the devil. They come to the great bend in the river at Nauvoo, Illinois, where the murdered Joseph Smith was buried and Brigham Young launched the great Mormon Exodus. They come to Hannibal, Missouri, to hang around the drowsy town where Sam Clemens dreamed of being a pilot on "the great Mississippi, the majestic, the magnificent Mississippi, rolling its mile-wide tide along, shining in the sun." Hordes come to Natchez every April for the annual "spring pilgrimage" to visit antebellum mansions. I don't know what such pilgrims seek within those lavish monuments to opulence. Do they ponder what it means to gain the world but lose one's soul? Or are so many still seduced by the "imitation gentry and shoddy manners and cheap emotions" of plantation life that Rhett Butler scorned in *Gone with the Wind*?

For there are dark sides of this river—stretches shrouded in mystery and haunted by histories of violence, enslavement, and death. Even Mark Twain, who mythologized the river, knew its darker side. Literary and cultural historian Thomas Ruys Smith puts it this way:

> Twain's vision of the Mississippi, in its youth at least, might persuasively be taken as a paradise. But he knew the river too well—had suffered on it too much—to think so simply. Dark intimations accompanied his river from the very start: murder and mortality in *Tom Sawyer*; slavery, deception, and violence in *Huck Finn;* the cruel and uncaring social world of the bitter *Pudd'nhead Wilson;* loss and deterioration in *Life on the Mississippi*. In one of his blackest moments, he imagined the afterlife of his childhood heroes: "Huck comes back, 60 years old, from nobody knows where—& crazy . . . Tom comes, at last, 60 from wandering the whole world & tends Huck, & together they talk the old times; both are desolate, life has been a failure, all that was lovable, all that was beautiful is under the mould. They die together."

Now in my sixties, I've come to the river—neither crazy nor despairing, as Twain was in his sixtieth year when his beloved daughter Susy died of meningitis. But I do seek consolation and enchantment.

Once, some years ago, I don't know exactly when, disillusion began to drain my spirit. For as long as I remember, books and nature have brought me solace. Both have been my refuge from—and engagement with—the world. But sometime—well before the summer of 2020—something had shifted. I'm not alone with feelings of disillusionment. Political theorist Jane Bennett refers to a "cultural narrative of disenchantment" in which "the prospects for loving life—or saying 'yes' to the world—are not good. What's to love about an alienated existence on a dead planet?" Many are languishing. The number of "deaths of despair" keeps rising.

I've made my living teaching college students the disciplines of literature and writing. I've witnessed the power of a book to change a life. There are those rare, transforming moments when the whole world is forever changed by the reading of a book. Richard Wright once said that for him, it was "not a matter of believing or disbelieving what I read, but of feeling something new, of being affected by something that made the look of the world different."

But there came a day when even the joy of teaching could not compensate for the disenchantment of a world diminishing daily before me. All around, I saw a decline in reading—in my own experience as well as among students. And that decline seems trivial against the disturbing disruptions of the living world—of ecosystems and social systems, of normalized violence and gross economic inequity. Each year, the evidence grows more ominous: not only a changing climate but vast populations of insects and amphibians fading away, along with many creatures that swim and fly and creep across the earth. The displacement of peoples and melting of glaciers, and above all, the stubborn refusal of humans to act wisely in the interest of all life, contribute to a global-wide sense that the earth is in crisis.

My good friend Paul Bogard introduced me to the term *solastalgia*, which he says is a complex emotional state informed by the concepts of both "solace" and "desolation." We associate solace with comfort and consolation in the face of distressing events. Desolation, on the other hand, comes with abandonment and loneliness. That very suffix, *-algia*, suggests pain or suffering—as in neuralgia, or fibromyalgia. Even nostalgia is itself a kind of "pain," which we experience as a longing to return—to a home, to an earlier time, to something familiar. *Solastalgia*, says Paul, is "the homesickness you have when you are still at home."

For me, some personal losses—the end of a marriage, the loss of a home, the fading of friendships, and my own aging body— magnified the *solastalgia*. It was in this condition I got a call from Don Postema, my philosopher friend, inviting me to a weekend retreat on Madeline Island.

Don and I had worked as colleagues and taught collaboratively for many years. He is now a bioethicist for a large hospital in Saint Paul, helping physicians navigate the ethical dilemmas of today's medical landscape. Don is soft-spoken and discerning, and an unfailing optimist. He is also a skilled carpenter and gourmet cook, attentive to the minute details of creating beauty, whether in wood or with food. Still, Don never takes himself too seriously and lightly excuses some mild eccentricities he inherited from his Dutch ancestors.

So, one late-summer afternoon, as we sat on the deck at Madeline Island, drinking a good pinot noir and looking out on Lake Superior, Don suggested I take to the river—not to the lakes of the north country I loved so well but to the big river, the mighty river, the Mississippi River.

"But I know nothing about the Mississippi," I countered. "Frankly, it scares me."

"Exactly," Don replied. "But I think it will teach you something."

"Teach me what?" I asked. "Should I take a canoe, float down the river from source to sea? What would that teach me?"

Don shrugged, reached for the bottle, and refilled our glasses. "Who knows?" he said. "But you are fascinated by the river, even if you avoid it. And, yes, I think it does scare you. You'd like to know more about it, but you haven't figured out how. So here's your chance."

"OK. Go on."

"Well, don't you love to teach *Huck Finn*? You once said it's the river that makes that novel great."

"Yeah, that was T. S. Eliot," I muttered, "not me."

But the suggestion Don planted that summer afternoon began to sprout into a genuine longing. I considered seriously what I might learn from the river and how I could learn it.

"Spending time by a river teaches us many things," says Thomas Moore, the Jungian psychologist and popular author of *Care of the Soul*. "One of them [is] the flow of life, its constant movement, and it's clear that an enchanted life demands an appreciation of this flow."

I have known what small streams can teach. The clear and muddy creeks of my childhood—those that trickled over the barren high plains of eastern Wyoming, drying up or swelling suddenly in late spring with the rush of snowmelt from distant mountains, or those that wandered lazily, like the sinuous Frenchman Creek, through the broad fields of southwestern Nebraska—carried in their seemingly insignificant flows the hints and suggestions of something greater. We waded them in summers and skated them in winters. My minister father did not baptize in these streams, but he could draw out biblical analogies easily—from Isaiah's prophetic "streams in the desert" to Jesus's promise of "rivers of living water." He cited often the image from the first psalm of one who, like a "tree planted beside streams of water," bears fruit, does not wither, and prospers. They served—these creeks and meandering streams—floating their spiritual freight lightly, then emptied themselves into the broader, deeper, and murkier rivers of my adulthood—the North Platte, the Missouri, and eventually the mighty Mississippi.

I approach the Mississippi, and all great rivers, real and imagined, with a kind of holy terror. In the faraway years of my childhood, on a bitterly cold Saturday night in mid-March, my grandmother Ginevra flung herself off the John A. Roebling Suspension Bridge into the wide Ohio River. Once, some years before my birth, she had tried to walk out into the river's cold current.

It was an unusually warm morning, January 20, 1944. On the radio, the news was all about the war and the bombing of Berlin. Grandmother Ginevra sent her daughters off to school and kissed my grandfather goodbye as he left the house for work. She turned the radio off, sat down at the kitchen table, and wrote a final farewell to the family. Then she walked a mile and a half to the edge of the Ohio River and kept on walking. Several hours later, my mother, then only eleven years old, came home for lunch and discovered the letter.

Edward Wright and Melvin Kessler were first and second mates on the steamboat *John W. Hubbard* that January morning when the stern-wheeler eased away from Cincinnati. They spotted my tiny grandmother bobbing in the current, but Grandmother did not want to be rescued. Wright and Kessler battled her resistance and pulled her from the river and onto the deck of the steamboat. So Grandmother Ginevra lived another dozen years—long enough to see her three daughters married, and for me to know her sorrowful face and trembling hands and touch the shiny waves of her raven hair.

The second time, a dozen years later, she simply leaped into the river, and the current took her in and bore her sad body down, down on its silent journey south, on toward its confluence with the mighty Mississippi.

I've been caught by the idea of "Riverness," perhaps in the way C. S. Lewis found himself caught by the idea of "Northernness" at a very early age. Lewis defined "Pure Northernness" as "a vision of huge, clear spaces hanging above the Atlantic in the endless twilight of Northern summer, remoteness, severity." Lewis never felt compelled to travel northward, but that vision would enchant him and linger with him all his life.

Like Lewis, I'm caught by an idea that comes largely from books: those ancient, dusky rivers Langston Hughes referred to— the Nile, the Congo, the Euphrates—and the biblical rivers of Jordan and Kishon. The mythical rivers of Acheron, Lethe, and Styx, and the musical names of the Yangtze, Amazon, Ganges, Danube, and Rhine still stir my imagination. Tolkien's mythic landscape of Middle-earth contains nearly eighty rivers; but his best known is the great river Anduin, flowing beside the Misty Mountains, past Mirkwood, coursing on through the realms of Gondor and Lorien.

The mythic dimensions of the Ohio River are magnified in Toni Morrison's *Beloved*. Gabriel García Márquez makes magic of Colombia's Magdalena River. In Joseph Conrad's novel *Heart of Darkness*, Marlow ponders the shape of the Congo, "a mighty big river, that you could see on the map, resembling an immense snake uncoiled, with its head in the sea, its body at rest curving afar over a vast country, and its tail lost in the depths of the land." In *A Passage to India*, E. M. Forster's old Mrs. Moore listens to Indian tales of crocodiles in the Ganges and of dead bodies floating down from Benares, and is moved to say, "What a terrible river! what a wonderful river!"

When I began writing this book, in the historic Pioneer Building of Saint Paul's Lowertown, I gazed each morning from my study window upon the terrible and wonderful river that is the Mississippi. I would take my four-year-old grandson to the rooftop patio on the seventeenth floor. Below, the landscape spreads out like a Little Golden Book's portrayal of an idealized city. We watched towboats pushing barges up and down the river. We watched long freight trains creeping up beside the bluffs from the switchyard to the southeast. The names of the trains were like music to his ears: Canadian Pacific, Union Pacific, and the Burlington Northern and Santa Fe. Some trains cross the river on the century-old lift bridge and turn toward the southwest, while others continue along the river's edge before heading north, away from the river. Upstream, we could see a paddleboat easing out from Harriet Island, followed by two long, narrow shells of university rowers, dipping their oars in unison.

My grandson pointed up to the enormous red numeral 1 flashing atop the First National Bank building next to the Pioneer Building. "1-s-т," he said, spelling out the symbol. "Why 1-s-т?" I replied with a joke I heard from a Saint Paul city planner. "1-s-т means First," I said. "And Saint Paul wants everyone to know it was here first, well before Minneapolis. So, they have a big red sign that says "First." He looked up at the flashing red sign for a bit, then turned to me. "You live in Saint Paul," he said. "I live in Minneapolis. Minneapolis is 2-s-т." He held up two fingers and studied them as if to be sure he was counting correctly. "Two is more than one," he gravely said. "Minneapolis is more than Saint Paul." I laughed and hugged him. "That it is," I said. Someday, I would tell him the tale of these twin cities and how they came to be such very different siblings.

This river has caught me, and I want to be near it, if not on it. "Once in his life," says N. Scott Momaday, "a man ought to concentrate his mind upon the remembered earth, I believe. He ought to give himself up to a particular landscape in his experience, to look at it from as many angles as he can, to wonder about it, to dwell upon it. He ought to imagine that he touches it with his hands at every season and listens to the sounds that are made upon it. He ought to imagine the creatures there and all the faintest motions of the wind. He ought to recollect the glare of noon and all the colors of dawn and dusk."

But how can I give myself to a landscape so immense and so variable? The most richly storied landscape in our nation has been—

a road to freedom and a route to bondage,
a commercial highway and natural flyway,
a force of nature and constructed channel,
a bringer of wealth and destroyer of health,
beautiful and treacherous,
uniting and dividing.

T. S. Eliot, who grew up in Saint Louis, called the Mississippi River a "strong brown god."

Of course, I could have surrendered to its flow, following the long procession of Americans who, like Abraham Lincoln in his youth, rafted down the Mississippi to New Orleans. It's one way to know the river, and for Lincoln, it gave him vital knowledge that would help him win the Civil War and preserve the nation. Going down the river is the archetypal American journey, mythologized by Mark Twain and reenacted and reinterpreted year after year in new and revealing ways.

But I want enchantment more than the thrill of adventure. It's not direction I need as much as connection. Enchantment, as Thomas Moore defines it, is "an ascendancy of the soul, a condition that allows us to connect, for the most part lovingly and intimately, with the world we inhabit." "As I'm using the term," says Jane Bennett, "enchantment entails a state of wonder, and one of the distinctions of this state is the temporary suspension of chronological time and bodily movement. To be enchanted, then, is to participate in a momentarily immobilizing encounter; it is to be transfixed, spellbound."

I want to be spellbound, to encounter the river, perhaps in ways as basic as Jesus instructed: consider the lilies, consider the ravens. I want to consider it from various perspectives, learn what I can of its mystery and allure. I want to be present with the river—not to navigate it nor to fish it but simply to be near it, to follow it and see what it has to show me.

The chapters that follow present a contemplative journey of time and place. This story does not trace a linear course from source to sea, as many river journeys do. Nor does it follow a chronological thread from beginning to end—for there are many beginnings! Its organization is thematic, informed by topography and memory. Its sequence is the river's unfolding as I have experienced its mystery. From the darkness of the river's gorge and the times in which I write, through the river's many confluences, around a great bend, from vistas atop the river bluffs, and of other recognitions beyond—this really is a story of falling in love, all over again—with the currents of time, the beauty of life, and the consolation of spirit.

BRIDGE

Looking into the Gorge

And forever and forever,
As long as the river flows,
As long as the heart has passions,
As long as life has woes;

The moon and its broken reflection
And its shadows shall appear . . .

—"The Bridge" by Longfellow

I MADE MY LIVING TEACHING LITERATURE AND WRITING TO college students, exploring with them the topographies of America's authors—the great plains and prairies of Cather and Erdrich, the mountains of Muir, the oceans of Melville, Jewett's country of pointed firs, and Hurston's Florida swamp land. Always, of course, there was the Mississippi River of Mark Twain. Sometimes, I fear, these literary landscapes were more real to me than any physical world they represent. The actual Mississippi River was not, for me, much more than a marker I crossed in driving from Saint Paul to Minneapolis, or something I admired while biking along Shepard Road. But my comfortable, suburban life came to a sudden end. I sold all that I had, moved into the city, and found myself living very near to the river.

Late one autumn, I stood on the bridge at midnight above Lock and Dam No. 1. My thoughts at that hour were dark, dark thoughts, and for many nights, I took myself there to sink into my sorrow and stare into the river. As I lingered and leaned in the warm glow of the streetlamps, the solid pillars and railing of the Ford Parkway Bridge spoke of sureness and strength.

At midnight, the whisper of water slipping over the dam is soothing and seductive. In time, my gaze was drawn outward, rather than downward. Upstream from this bridge, the river pours through the Mississippi River Gorge, sliding beneath the arches of the Lake Street–Marshall Avenue Bridge. Downstream, just past the dam, the foam-flecked water divides around a small, barren island, then bends out of sight, going on past the tiny mouth of Hidden Falls Creek, where it makes a sharper bend and continues on to merge with the silt-laden Minnesota River beneath the bluffs of old Fort Snelling, a sacred confluence known as Bdote.

From the Ford Parkway Bridge, I could see, on the east bank, signs of new development where the old Ford plant once stood. Here Ford once mined the river's deposits of pure, white silica to make its glass for automobiles; Ford drew its hydropower from the river's flow to make its Model Ts and Model As, and in the end, its Ranger trucks. High up on the west bank, above Lock and Dam No. 1, sprawls the campus of the old veterans home, constructed in the Gilded Age to shelter aging Civil War vets. Here I stood between two worlds. The streets of Highland Park spread to the east; and to the west, the green hills of Minnehaha Park and its legendary falls. Minnehaha Creek bends around behind the veterans home and empties into the Mississippi River.

From this point above the dam, a crow flying northwest and a crow flying northeast would arrive about the same time in downtown Minneapolis and downtown Saint Paul. These notations of cartography and culture mean little in themselves; but they signify my starting point, the coordinates of a new beginning.

1

It's February 27, one of those heavy, late afternoons when the snow sifts down from leaden skies. We are in the depth of a Minnesota winter—the New Year now is not so new and spring so far away. "Today is the birthday of the poet Henry Wadsworth Longfellow." The voice from Minnesota Public Radio interrupts the stream of music I'd been enjoying and distracts me from my reading. I reach for the remote, but before I can mute the voice and resume my reading, these lines from Longfellow fill the room:

> *You who love a nation's legends,*
> *Love the ballads of a people,*
> *That like voices from afar off*
> *Call to us to pause and listen.*

So, I pause and listen, and the voice murmurs on. And soon I am dusting off a leather-bound volume of Longfellow's poems that once belonged to my grandmother Ginevra.

Near the edge of the Longfellow neighborhood, on the west bank of the Mississippi River Gorge, sits the Longfellow Grill, looking out onto the Lake Street Bridge. Some impulse leads me to go there for an early supper, book in hand.

Longfellow never saw this part of the country—though he tried to imagine its beauty and generated names and legends that have, for better or worse, become part of our public consciousness. When Minnesota became a state in 1858, Longfellow's "Song of Hiawatha" had become enormously popular, prompting many of the place-names in the neighborhood—Hiawatha Avenue, Minnehaha Falls, Lake Nokomis. Just a few miles south of the Longfellow Grill stands a two-thirds replica of Longfellow's Cambridge home, built in 1907 by a fanatic fishmonger and Longfellow fan, Robert Fremont Jones. I settle into a booth and order a black bean burger and beer; my server is cordial and attentive but has no idea who the person named Longfellow was.

I've hidden my affection for that old fireside poet, and rarely do I introduce his work to my students. He was enormously popular in his time—as popular as Bono or Bob Dylan or Prince have been to mine. A professor of modern languages at Harvard, he led a privileged life, and his poems, however tender and well crafted, reflect a carelessness born of privilege. He mixed up names and legends from various First Nations, and apparently took, without acknowledgment, ideas from the work of Jane Schoolcraft, now considered America's first native writer of literary art. Her Ojibwe name was a poem in itself—Bamewawagezhikaquay—which signified the sound of stars rushing through the sky.

Nevertheless, that bearded old poet had a tender heart, and endeavored to give a voice to the voiceless. In one astonishing poem, he imagined the bones of the millions who vanished in the Atlantic during the slave trade's Middle Passage:

> *They glare from the abyss;*
> *They cry, from unknown graves,*
> *"We are the Witnesses!"*

Not until 1987—when Lucille Clifton described the Atlantic as a sea of bones, a bridge of ivory "connecting whydah and new york," and Toni Morrison conjured up the ghost of "Beloved" to speak for the lost women of the Middle Passage—had any other poet commemorated that "disremembered" nation of witnesses.

Henry had known great pain. In 1861, he watched his beloved second wife, Fanny Appleton, go up in flames. Late one night, she burst into his study, her gauzy Victorian dress all aflame. "Henry!" she cried. He smothered the flames with a rug, burning his own hands and face; but her burns were severe, and she died the next day. Then, late in 1863, at the darkest time of the American Civil War, Henry got word that his son Charles had been critically wounded in battle. So he sat down and composed the line, "I heard the bells on Christmas Day," and pulled himself back from the brink of despair.

Now, sitting in the Longfellow Grill on the west bank of the Mississippi River, I leaf through Longfellow's earliest poems, *Voices of the Night.* I think of him as a patron saint for insomniacs. The metered lines work on me like incantations:

> *I heard the trailing garments of the Night*
> *Sweep through her marble halls!*

Longfellow was acquainted with the night, or "the haunted chambers of the night," as he put it. Ghosts and shadows lurk in his lines—not the Gothic shapes of Poe and Lovecraft but the familiar haunts of homes and fireplaces, thoughts of "what might have been," and the residue of dreams—what he called "the long-lost ventures of the heart."

In "The Beleaguered City," he retold the story of a spectral army encamped on the banks of the Moldau River in the old city of Prague. At midnight, so the ancient legend goes, this ghostly army besieged the city until the cathedral bells tolled, calling its citizens to prayer. To Henry, this image represented the hauntings of life:

> *Encamped beside Life's rushing stream,*
> *In Fancy's misty light,*
> *Gigantic shapes and shadows gleam*
> *Portentous through the night.*

Upon its midnight battle-ground
The spectral camp is seen,
And, with a sorrowful, deep sound,
Flows the River of Life between.

But the poem that hooks me now is the one he simply titled, "The Bridge."

I stood on the bridge at midnight,
As the clocks were striking the hour,
And the moon rose o'er the city,
Behind the dark church-tower.

Still grieving the death of his first wife, Mary, Henry had pursued the wealthy and resistant Fanny Appleton. A young Harvard professor and aspiring poet, Henry nightly walked from Cambridge to Boston to see her, crossing the Charles River and pausing on the bridge to gaze at the moon and its "broken reflection." After seven persistent years, Fanny accepted his proposal. In this poem, composed shortly after they married, Henry recalled his own dark thoughts he had while standing on the bridge, and he pondered the sorrow of care-encumbered thousands who "have crossed the bridge since then."

If you go to Harvard today, you can drive across the Longfellow Bridge from Cambridge to Boston, or you can walk across the new and elegant Frances Appleton Pedestrian Bridge stretching out beside it and gaze at the moon in the Charles River. From where I sit in the Longfellow Grill on the west bank of the Mississippi River, I see cars and pedestrians moving slowly in both directions across the beautiful Lake Street–Marshall Avenue Bridge. On the other side of the river hangs the moon, not quite full, behind a thin curtain of clouds. The snow has stopped.

There is magic in this poet, a voice from a far-off time, calling me to pause, to listen, to attend to where I am. The Charles River, Henry said, taught him "many a lesson, deep and long." I wonder what the Mississippi River might have to teach me? I close my book, pay the tab, and step out into the night.

I stand alone on the Lake Street Bridge and gaze across the frozen expanse of the Mississippi River Gorge. Below, the ice appears fractured and whorled, and a few broken spots reveal dark water beneath. Up the gorge to the north, I see the dark shapes of downtown Minneapolis; to the south, bright pink-orange lights outline the Ford Parkway Bridge. On either side of the river, the steep slopes bristle with bare trees, and through them, I see the lights of the cars on the bluff tops, moving silently up and down the East River Parkway and up and down the West River Parkway. It is not difficult to imagine a spectral army lurking here on both sides of the gorge, moving silently up the frozen river at midnight to besiege Minneapolis.

Through the remaining weeks of winter, I spend evenings in the library, reading about the Mississippi River's history. I discover, as Joseph Conrad once said of the river Thames, "this also has been one of the dark places of the earth." Darkness fell on the Mississippi with those European explorers who sought to possess it. La Salle, that first European to travel the Mississippi, was ambushed in 1687 by his own crew near the river's mouth; his body has never been found.

On old maps, I trace the ghostly shapes of the Mississippi's abandoned riverbeds and the once-thriving river towns that have vanished. I locate the Trail of Tears State Park, marking the place where thousands of Cherokee were forced across the river during the brutal winter of 1838 and 1839. I read about (and eventually visit) Fort Pillow on the Chickasaw bluffs north of Memphis, where Confederate lieutenant general Nathan Bedford Forrest massacred several hundred African American soldiers in April of 1864. After the war, Forrest became the first grand wizard of the Ku Klux Klan. I study pictures of the spectral remains of once-opulent sugar plantations in Louisiana. I learn that hundreds of skeletal remains of steamboats lie buried in the Mississippi's muddy graveyard.

Stories of ghosts and hauntings course freely throughout the Mississippi's dark history; there are houses and hotels up and down the river that are said to be haunted. On the Illinois shore near Grand Tower, I've walked atop a rocky outcropping called the Devil's Backbone, once dreaded for its evil spirits, its turbulent rapids, and its river bandits. To countless slaves, sold up and down the river, the Mississippi was nothing less than the valley of the shadow of death.

2

Spring arrived, and I yearned for the river itself—to touch it and to ride its current. On a cloudless morning in early June, I joined a flotilla of kayaks and canoes for a leisurely paddle down a stretch of the Mississippi River. Several dozen urban adventurers who had met online gathered in Fridley, the east bank river town just north of Minneapolis. Most of us were experienced paddlers of Minnesota's lakes and streams; few of us had ever ventured out onto the mighty Mississippi.

Our leader was a relaxed, young man who instructed us in launching and safety and told us how to navigate along the west bank and through the locks. Several kayaks sprouted flags; they would be our designated "spotters" and would come to the aid of any craft in distress. His voice was calm and assuring—just follow the river, he told us, and get out at Harriet Island.

I don't remember seeing very much of the city, nor much of the shore life either, as we adjusted to the pull of the river's current, maintaining a proper distance from the other kayaks and canoes. But I do remember the bridges—each span so different and all so lovely. We passed in wonder beneath the graceful arcs of the Lowry Avenue Bridge, soaring above us like handles on some gigantic Easter basket. That bridge had only recently opened, and its broad supporting piers were also new. Then, in quick succession, we passed beneath a railroad bridge, the Broadway Bridge, the Plymouth Bridge, another railroad bridge, then glided beneath the majestic Hennepin Avenue Bridge in the heart of the city. As we floated through the Third Avenue Bridge, we saw the great doors to the Upper Saint Anthony Falls lock swing open to receive us. And when all of the kayaks and canoes were inside the lock, and the doors had closed behind us, we felt more like a collection of bathtub toys than a flotilla of explorers. We held on to the ropes as instructed and talked in low tones as the water dropped beneath us. This would be the only time I would pass through that lock, for Congress permanently closed it in 2015 to halt the spread of invasive carp.

Just beyond the old Stone Arch Bridge, we glanced back over our shoulders to the dam, then ahead toward the Lower Saint Anthony Falls lock. The water was roiled now, and we let it carry us, using our paddles only to stay steady and to avoid colliding with another. High above us on the right, the Guthrie's "endless bridge" jutted from its dark blue building. We entered the lower lock, and the water dropped again. Before us stretched the new I-35W bridge, where, on a warm August evening a few years before, the old steel structure had collapsed in rush-hour traffic, dropping cars and trucks and slabs of concrete and steel into the river. A bus of schoolchildren teetered on the edge. Thirteen people died, and many more were injured.

The turbulence caught us coming out of the second lock, flinging kayaks and canoes against each other. Several capsized. And then, just as quickly, the water calmed. The river bent away to the right and there we were, drifting serenely through the University of Minnesota campus.

On the east bank, the stainless-steel walls of the Weisman Art Museum caught the morning sun and scattered its blazing light. I've been told the building represents a waterfall and fish, but I'm unable to see it. From the Weisman, the Washington Avenue Bridge connects to the east and west banks of the university campus. Pedestrians and cyclists, cars, buses, and a light-rail train cross over on two levels of the maroon bridge. It was from this bridge many years ago—when I was in college and beginning to study poetry—that the celebrated, tormented poet John Berryman leaped to his death.

With the excitement of the second lock behind us, my partner and I fell silent, and our paddling slowed. We passed the sprawling East River Flats on our left and the Bohemian Flats on our right and then, it seemed to us, the sun began to grow very warm. Kayaks and canoes drifted apart, and the shouting and banter between them faded. We passed beneath the I-94 bridge and the Franklin Avenue Bridge. And then, we entered a great stillness. Noise from the city almost completely disappeared.

Horace Cleveland, the great American landscape architect, called this remarkable stretch of river the "lungs" of the city. "No artist who has any appreciation of natural beauty," he wrote to the Minneapolis Park Board in 1883, "would presume to do more than touch with reverent hands the features whose charms suggest their own development." Some of that natural beauty remains—the Mississippi River Gorge is now part of a much larger recreational area of the National Park Service; but the hands that touched the gorge over the decades were not always reverent, and many of the features that charmed Horace Cleveland are no longer visible.

There's a stillness in the gorge, an eerie sense of enchantment, as if something has been put on hold or is holding its breath.

I've caught a glimpse of this lost world in the archives of the Minnesota History Center. Ferdinand Richardt's 1857 painting of the falls presents a marvelously detailed vista, looking upstream toward the falls across a broad expanse of rapids and rocks. In the distance are the carefully rendered buildings of a fledgling city, and on either side of the stream, bluffs rise, built from layers of sandstone, shale, and limestone deposited by the vast Ordovician seas of more than four hundred million years ago. What an awesome sound those rapids must have made, echoing through this exquisite little canyon. The gorge itself was carved quite recently, by geological standards. Eight thousand years ago, perhaps, the falls would have been as far downstream as present-day Saint Paul. Water rushing over the limestone edge of the falls eroded the sandstone beneath it, causing the limestone shelf to break off in jagged pieces. And the process would repeat, driving the falls steadily upstream to their current location. It's likely the falls would have kept migrating, but their progress was stopped in 1870 when a dam was built to harness the river's hydropower. Then, in the early twentieth century, these "lungs" of the city began to fill when another dam was built.

My companion, in the prow, turned and called me from my reverie. We were drifting toward the east side of the river. Shouts of laughter came from the west side; several of our companions had pulled their canoes up onto a bank of white sand. They were wading and splashing. But our canoe drifted toward a straight line of concrete bollards protruding from the water like giant mushrooms—mooring posts atop the wall of the old Meeker Island Lock and Dam. Had I been braver, I might have stepped out of the canoe onto the top of the wall, only inches beneath the river's surface. I stared at the ghostly outline of the old wall sinking into the murky depth beneath me. I put my hand on one of the bollards to steady myself.

I've read about the short life of this Meeker Island Lock and Dam. Local historian John Anfinson says it was the very first dam to straddle the Mississippi River. Built in 1907 just north of the Lake Street–Marshall Avenue Bridge, the Meeker Island lock was used only for a few years before it was abandoned for the much larger Lock and Dam No. 1 farther downstream. The Meeker Island dam was removed, but one wall of the lock remains. Waters rising behind the higher dam formed what is now called Pool One. Through Pool One, boats and barges could easily reach Minneapolis; and in time, Meeker Island itself disappeared. But with the closing of the upper falls lock in 2015, barges no longer venture up this far.

It truly seemed a mysterious realm. No ghost armies were encamped along the river; but the trees on either side jostled and crowded at the river's edge. Were there houses or buildings or docks or anything else to humanize this stretch, it might have felt like a more welcoming place.

We drifted on, gliding beneath the Lake Street–Marshall Avenue Bridge where I'd stood the previous winter and wondered what the river might teach me, and then through the Ford Parkway Bridge where I had stood so many times at midnight. By the time we finished locking through Lock and Dam No. 1, all of us were beginning to feel like river rats. We slid past the enormous cliffs of Fort Snelling and marveled as the Minnesota River poured its earthier stream into our river. And then we leaned into our paddles, no longer drifting, driving ourselves on to reach the city with the cathedral on the hill.

I'm trying to recall details as we neared Saint Paul but have only bare outlines of memory: the walls of the gorge that seemed to withdraw and the lush, wild expanse of Lilydale Park spreading out before us. And then, just before we came to Harriet Island, we passed under the High Bridge, arching far above us. Its alluring height has been a fatal siren call to many in despair. The bridge has recently been renovated with suicide-prevention fences installed. But before that, there were nearby residents, I've been told, who kept watch for any care-encumbered person who might be standing on the High Bridge at midnight.

Harriet Island was a celebratory landing, and we ended our journey with rejoicing. Kayaks and canoes were pulled from the river and spread out on the grass. Everyone arrived safely; we congratulated each other on the great shared adventure. Those few who collided and capsized were already magnifying their tale, like the stories of fishers that grow with each telling. After high fives and handshakes, we loaded up and headed home.

3

Through the indolent days of midsummer, I ride along the Mississippi River bikeways, up one side and cross over, then back down the other side. I'm drawn by the beauty of the bluff top and the tree-lined boulevards. There are ongoing efforts by conservationists to restore what can be restored. But it's fraught with tension, too; park benches, once so lovingly and strategically placed to overlook the river, now face into a dense curtain of green.

The gorge in midsummer seems wild and enchanted. There is a Hawthornian feel to these sheltered woods. From the West River Parkway, a narrow trail drops sharply down through the undergrowth and takes me straight to the river's edge. A fox, then a coon, seem untroubled by my presence. On the east side of the river, I slip into the gorge through the university flats, following an asphalt path south from the campus. Runners and bikers dodge past. Here, on the city side of the path, sheer layers of limestone, shrouded in green, rise up to the parkway atop the bluff. On the river side of the path, trees lean in toward the river—slippery elm, basswood, black ash, and maple. Some of the trees have fallen.

Beneath the I-94 bridge, a narrow, elevated walkway runs along the east bank, right at the river's edge. I loiter here above the dark waters and try to imagine the music of the gorge before the dams came. If the dams could be removed, would the fish and the mussels and the vanished aquatic wildlife return? Could the accumulated silt of the century—an estimated 1.5 million cubic yards—ever be washed away? Would the groaning of the gorge break into song?

I realize I am still grieving, staring expectantly, waiting—for what, I'm not sure. For inspiration? For words? For the spirit to descend and breathe life into me, as the stifled lungs of the gorge are yearning for breath? The trees move closer as the sun drops behind them. The shadows darken. The stillness unnerves me.

One other summer day, I walk with my bicycle down a paved trail from the bluff top to the site of the old Meeker Island lock. The paved trail ends, and I lean my bike against a tree and make my way to the water's edge. It's no place to linger, but I stand there anyway, kicking at the sandy soil and contemplating the bollards that mark the submerged wall. Everything feels close here. Rivulets run down the limestone wall behind me; all around, the trees and the undergrowth lean in toward the river. In the stillness, I gaze through their branches, hoping to spot an eagle or a hawk overhead. There is nothing but blue sky.

The heaviness of summer lifts, and autumn's beauty emerges. I bike along the river almost daily and often in late afternoon. The walls of the gorge, uniformly green in the summer, now burst with the distinctive colors of the maples and oaks, cottonwoods and birches. Nearly a year has now passed since I stood on a bridge at midnight and listened to the whisper of the water slipping over the dam.

4

A chilling murder took place on the rocks below the ruins of the old Meeker Island lock. It was a Saturday night in 1914—November 28, to be precise—the last day of ordinary time, by the church's liturgical calendar. The next day would be sacred, the beginning of Advent.

Mary Fridley stood where the bluff is highest and the drop the sharpest. Her husband's Model T had broken down that night, apparently, on the East River Parkway, and her husband and his ne'er-do-well friend were bent over the open hood as they talked together in low tones. The preceding Thursday had been the warmest Thanksgiving Day on record. Now, a great chill had descended with the night, and Mary drew her shawl tightly around her. Her dog, Chum, frisked among the grasses near the edge of the bluff.

Mary Fridley was the granddaughter of the man who'd founded Fridley, that east bank river town just north of Minneapolis. By all accounts, Mary was a small, plain, thirty-five-year-old woman whose father adored her and from whom she had just received a small fortune. As Mary stood on that bluff in the shadows, she was pondering how best to use her inherited money. She had been talking over Thanksgiving about funding a children's home or building a shelter for women; but her husband, Fred, an unsuccessful salesman, had argued bitterly with her. And then, to her surprise and delight, Fred and his ne'er-do-well friend decided to take her out to a show on Saturday night, followed by a leisurely ride along the East River Parkway.

Driving south from the Franklin Avenue Bridge, the car climbed steadily upward until, just before the Lake Street–Marshall Avenue Bridge, at the highest point above the gorge, the motor died. Across the river, the sky was darkening into a deep purple; high on her left, Mary saw the yellow lights of Model Ts moving ghostlike across the arches of the bridge. Then, a cold wind came rushing up out of the gorge, and Mary felt herself falling.

The story the salesman spun for the police appeared on the front page of the next morning's Minneapolis *Sunday Tribune*, November 29: Mary had tragically fallen from the bluff to the rocks below, trying to rescue her dog, Chum, who had slipped over the edge. The narrow column reporting her death was squeezed between two larger stories—one on the toddler John Jacob Astor VI (who only two years earlier had survived the *Titanic* disaster that drowned his famous father), and another report about a massive deployment of British troops to the western coast of France. So, Mary's murder slipped through easily as an accident; the wicked husband collected her money and promptly married his mistress. Had it not been for his greed, the foul deed might never have been exposed.

Within a year, Fred filed suit against the Minneapolis Park Board for negligence in Mary's death. Mary's suspicious father hired a detective to uncover the truth. Poor Mary's bones, having lain in the earth for a year, were dug up. Her battered skull, brought into the courtroom, corroborated the damning testimony of the accomplice.

It seems that the two murderers, having flung Mary Fridley from the bluff that fateful night, descended and found her lying on the rocks below—not dead but moaning, her legs drawn up to her chin. The husband, testified the accomplice, calmly picked up a boulder and smashed in her skull. Although he denied it, the evidence said otherwise, and he would spend the rest of his life in a Stillwater prison. Mary Fridley's bones were reinterred in Lakewood Cemetery. On a brisk autumn night, high on that bluff above the gorge, I have paused where Mary Fridley stood and listened to the moaning wind, and I am sure I heard the whimpering of a dog and a woman's worried cry, "Chum. Chum."

5

The gorge is a land of shades. I go there to listen—for, dammed and silenced though it has become, the gorge *does* speak, in slow, mournful tones from the basement of time. Like the Greek heroes who descended into their land of the shades, I'd like to bring back something life-giving.

Much of this seven-mile stretch, from the falls to Bdote, is hidden, unseen by the city. Behind the trees are walls of sandstone and limestone, the stratified records of warm Paleozoic seas, teeming with life that covered this land for millions of years, long before dinosaurs, long before any of the five great extinctions and the surges of life that followed each extinction. Ancient seas, transgressing and regressing, deposited enormous amounts of sand, layers of mud, then a steady accumulation of marine life—cephalopods, crinoids, trilobites, brachiopods, clams, corals, snails—all living and dying and sinking to the seabed—slowly building up this Platteville Limestone, a monument of ancient time through which the river runs. The cutting of the gorge, by comparison, was done in a mere moment of geological time.

From recorded observations going back to 1680, Minnesota's first geologist, Newton Horace Winchell, calculated the migration of the falls up the river gorge at about eight thousand years. A later geologist, H. E. Wright, Jr., confirmed Winchell's estimate as "remarkably close to the radiocarbon dates for these events."

I contemplate these markings of time, the vast deposits from ancient seas and the river's yawning split. I feel like I've fallen into some ancient, disturbing text—a mysterious, sacred script with the awful power to swallow me. Here's a buried lock between locks, an abandoned passage within a closed passage, layers upon layers, the accumulations of waters and the carving away by other waters; and beneath it all are the silent, ancient rocks.

Yi-Fu Tuan, the famous geographer, defined space and place as a dialectic in which we live and move and have our being. "Place is security, space is freedom: we are attached to the one and long for the other," he writes. "Space and place are basic components of the lived world; we take them for granted."

Dammed at both ends, the gorge seems neither a space nor a place. "Dammed at both ends and cursed in the middle," as Henry Thoreau said of the Concord River in 1860. Dammed at both ends—a sign of the times in which I now find myself. I study the still stretch of water before me, and the bridge overhead, reaching from bluff top to bluff top. No one dwells here; they pass through or cross over. The elements of the gorge are not those of the lived world. But if I attend, lean in, and listen closely, I wonder if they might point me toward some new life as yet *un*lived.

I come back to poor Mary Fridley and her unrealized dreams falling with her into the gorge. I ponder this dammed-up stream with its silt steadily building behind Lock and Dam No. 1, the doors of the Upper Saint Anthony Falls lock now permanently bolted, and between these two dams, the submerged lock of the abandoned Meeker Island dam. On either side of the stream, the trees, leaning in, listen for the stopped-up music of the gorge.

I, too, lean and listen for what it is within me that remains silent and locked. What music might there be, waiting to be voiced, even as the stifled lungs of the gorge yearn for breath? The trees edge closer. The shadows darken, and I flee.

6

At the east end of the Cappelen (Franklin Avenue) Bridge—below a concrete arch supporting the parkway, and above a stone embankment reinforcing the bluff—rivulets of water seep down the limestone face. This is all that remains of an exquisite waterfall that once poured from the top of the bluff into the Mississippi River a hundred feet below. I had not known about these falls until I came across a slim book called *Riverside Reveries*, composed in 1928 by Otto F. Schussler, a Minneapolis physician. Dr. Schussler loved to walk across this bridge with his wife, Edith, pausing at the midpoint to listen and to gaze up and down the river gorge.

When the Cappelen Memorial Bridge replaced the older, iron truss bridge in 1923, it was one of several stunning, concrete arch bridges to be built across the gorge in the early twentieth century. The Cappelen Bridge, at that time, contained the longest concrete arch in the world. The famous Bridal Veil Falls on the east bank, however, had vanished, a casualty of the city's encroachment.

Otto Schussler traveled a great deal in the Mississippi River Gorge. He and Edith often walked a loop "from the hospital down the west bank of the river, across the Cappelen Bridge, up the east bank to the Washington Avenue Bridge over to the west bank again and back to the hospital." Students of the nearby Fairview School of Nursing also walked this loop, and so Dr. Schussler dedicated his *Riverside Reveries* to a Fairview graduate confined to her home by a lingering illness.

Whatever comfort or healing these essays might have brought that convalescing nurse is impossible to know. Not much is known about the doctor, either, who wrote so tenderly about the river gorge. He composed some humorous essays, too, and a book of Alaskan stories, called *Pills*; but Dr. Schussler was modest about his literary endeavors.

Some years after Otto's death, his wife, Edith Schussler, published her memoir about their early years of working at a frontier hospital in Montana. She recalled her husband's blue eyes and neatly groomed Vandyke beard, his easy laughter, and "that little low whistle that I always knew meant that he had something to tell me that he was sure would not meet with my approval."

Now, nearly a century later, as I labor on my own riverside reveries, I'm grateful to have found this gentle guide who wrote so well of time and place—of the Mississippi River Gorge, particularly, and of changes witnessed and beauty perceived. He wrote about walking—along the river's edges and across its bridges—and about pausing on those bridges to look and to listen. His contemplative voice speaks health, especially as framed by two reveries—one near the book's opening and one near its end.

In his essay of August 5, 1927, Schussler recalls the beautiful falls he had known in his youth: "This deep gash into the great limestone ledge was cut by a busy little creek which up to about fifteen years ago threw itself into the Mississippi here and formed, at a distance of perhaps two hundred feet back from the river's edge, a particularly picturesque and pleasing waterfall." Then, he offers this brief study of enchantment he experienced on the earlier iron bridge:

> In those simple but (I believe) better days, before the advent of
> trolley cars and automobiles, this romantic "Falls" was well out
> in the country, and the iron bridge (which you will remember

did service here until about four years ago) was by no means an over-crowded thorofare [*sic*]. It was in fact seldom burdened with more than one slowly moving horse-drawn vehicle at a time. The noise and din that is constant upon the great concrete structure which has lately replaced it was entirely wanting then and the reverberating but restful call of the little cascade could be plainly heard upon the old bridge at a point well beyond midstream. Those were more leisurely times than we are now living in, at least the methods of travel then in use were more leisurely than those in vogue today, and they that crossed the bridge seemed somehow always to have time to give old Dobbin a few minutes in which to "blow" while they feasted eyes and ears upon the satisfying sights and sounds which this bewitching sylvan nook afforded. I think we can all understand their inclination to loiter here. There is something about a waterfall that is irresistibly alluring, a sort of magical charm it holds which throws an enchantment over those who venture near it and engenders in their minds a reminiscent mood of a vague and enthralling kind.

Enchantment came readily then—evoked by the leisurely times, the waterfall's alluring charm, and the inclination to loiter. But what of the noisier, concrete Cappelen Bridge, and the extinguishing of the falls?

Nine months later (May 5, 1928), near the end of *Riverside Reveries*, Schussler again describes his regular evening stroll with Edith across the newer Cappelen Bridge. And, as before, they linger:

As nearly as may be, we endeavor to arrive upon the bridge at sundown; and although it not infrequently happens that cloudy skies obscure the sinking sun even so, "the time, the place and the girl" serve as reminders of other sunsets seen and enjoyed here in the past, and I derive not a little pleasure from my reminiscences.

Having loitered on the bridge till the last lingering tints of pink and gold have faded from the evening sky, we continue our walk. From a slight rise of ground on the east bank, just above the now defunct Bridal Veil Falls, a particularly fine view of the bridge and its reflection in the water may be had at this time of day. The great semi-circular arches are now converted into complete circles by unison with their inverted images which hang suspended in the broad river. A more exquisitely beautiful picture than the one presented upon a calm, clear evening in early summer could not be dreamed of.

What I appreciate most about *Riverside Reveries* is its hearty effort for wholeness. Schussler does not ignore the environmental loss—he laments "the melancholy drip, drip of the puny trickle of water falling over the rim of the Bridal Veil ledge"—but neither does he express resignation. His words encourage me to continue nurturing memory and relationships, to maintain the daily rounds and routines, to shift perspective as needed, and to keep looking for the circles of wholeness joining the natural and constructed elements of the world.

CONFLUENCE
Where Waters Come Together

Here is America's heartbeat:
two spinning rivers writhe in circles,
charge into the watery labyrinth:
another beat, another maddened run.

—"The Confluence" by Peter Neil Carroll

1

ONG AGO, A YOUNG WOMAN AND A MAN MET NEAR
Bdote, the sacred confluence of the Minnesota and
Mississippi Rivers. She was Mdewakanton Dakota,
raised in a village near the shores of Bde Maka Ska
in what is now the western part of Minneapolis. He
descended from European immigrants and grew up in western New York, in the "burned over" region between the Fin-
ger Lakes and Lake Ontario. He'd come to Minnesota with his
brother, in his teens.

The woman's name was Naginowenah, meaning "Spirit of
the Moon." Her mother was the sister of Chief Wabasha, and
her father was the brother of Mahpiya Wicasta, or Cloud Man,
the village chief. The name of the man was Prescott—Philander Prescott—from the classical *Philandros*, meaning "lover of
humanity." These two would spend forty years together; but in
the end, both suffered from the violence that erupted from the
collision of their cultures.

I knew nothing of their story when I came to the river town
of Prescott not so long ago. I had thought to travel down the
Great River Road along the eastern route, beginning in Prescott,
Wisconsin, across the river from Red Wing, Minnesota.

When you cross into Prescott, you pass a clock tower first built in 1867, and rebuilt several times since. Cafés, bars, and shops along Broad Street invite you to linger. Here the Saint Croix River, flowing briskly down from Wisconsin's north country, butts into the slower, muddier Mississippi; and where the rivers collide, a long, narrow peninsula has formed from sand carried by the swifter flowing stream. This peninsula, Point Douglas, is now a rustic little park, perfect for a picnic or for loafing on the grass. You can watch the yachts and fishing boats come and go from one stream to the other. Above the point of confluence, the drawbridge and the lift bridge carry cars and trains between Wisconsin and Minnesota.

A mile south of the town, on a bluff above the river, stands the Great River Road Visitor and Learning Center. It's a lovely space, built of stone, wood, and glass, and surrounded by prairie grasses, flowers, and long, enchanting views. Looking north through the hazy stillness, you can almost see where the waters come together.

Inside the center, you'll learn about the natural and cultural history of these two rivers. You'll grasp the ecosystem basics of river-bluff prairies and of river-bottom forests. You can learn about thirty-eight species of mussels found in the Saint Croix River, or how the Mississippi River provides a flyway for half of the nation's migrating birds. You'll gain perspectives on the ancient history of mound-builders, and the more recent histories of Ojibwe and Dakota life along the two rivers. And there are maps and guidebooks to help you visualize the Great River Road that stretches all the way down to the Gulf, marked by the green-and-white pilot-wheel icons.

I soaked it in and envisioned being that traveler to the Gulf. I carry a peculiar recollection from my childhood reading—an image of the house of the interpreter in John Bunyan's antique allegory, *The Pilgrim's Progress*. "This Book will make a Traveler of thee," Bunyan promised, and it did—stirring my youthful imagination and giving me nightmares! This interpreter's house, however—free from any allegory or dogma—provided direction for another kind of pilgrimage along the river.

But I wouldn't become that traveler yet. A brief conversation with the "interpreter" of the visitor's center—a woman of middle years and persistent curiosity—turned me back upstream to Prescott. "Spend some time up near the confluence," she said to me. And so I did.

2

To see precisely where the Saint Croix River meets the Mississippi, it's best to go a bit downstream, by boat or by foot, along the Wisconsin side of the Mississippi. Between the river and the railroad runs a narrow strip of land with a walkway and marina, and an imposing string of condominiums. A block or two away, at the Twisted Oak Coffee House, I picked up a cup and croissant, then went back and perched on a picnic table above the moored boats.

There's something about a confluence that invites contemplation—a bit like facing a fork in the road. "Two roads diverged in a yellow wood," begins a famous poem by Robert Frost. It's a staple of literature classrooms, but still has power to set its readers thinking of choices they have made and how they made them. Metaphors of roads and of streams speak to the soul. Roads diverge, streams converge. Both kinds of juncture—the parting of ways and the joining of ways—can lead you to think of time, but with differing angles of vision. To stand where a road divides is to peer ahead and ponder "how way leads on to way." To stand where streams converge is to wonder how things have come together. It can be a bit mystical! As Whitman wrote:

To me the converging objects of the universe perpetually flow,
All are written to me, and I must get what the writing means.

I've been thinking about confluences—of how people, throughout human history, have gathered where streams come together. At "the Forks" in downtown Winnipeg, where the Assiniboine River meets the Red, people have been gathering for more than six millennia. Confluences are good places for commerce, in the best sense of the word, where goods are traded and ideas exchanged. In Pittsburgh, the Monongahela meets the Allegheny to form the great Ohio River. In India, two glacier-fed streams—the Bhagirathi and Alaknanda—converge in Devprayag to form the sacred river Ganges; and the Ganges and Yamuna are said to join the metaphysical river Sarasvati, near Allahabad, to form the holy Triveni Sangam.

For indigenous Americans, confluences have been sacred. In Arizona, where the Colorado River meets the Little Colorado, on the eastern side of the Grand Canyon, the confluence is sacred to both Navaho and Hopi. I once heard a Navaho explain its sacredness this way: "The Colorado is a female principle, and the Little Colorado a male principle. Where the emerald waters of the Colorado meet the turquoise waters of the Little Colorado, a foamy froth is generated, representing life's beginnings." But the dominant forces of American culture show little interest in the sacred. In 2017, after many years of resistance, the Navaho nation successfully stopped one developer's plan to build a

mega-resort and tramway that would have desecrated the confluence of the Colorado and Little Colorado.

Here, in Prescott, I watched a solitary fisherman, just off
the point, maneuvering his boat away from the Saint Croix's
shimmering water into the slower, thicker stream of the Mississippi River. Above the point, the heavy, iron railroad bridge
began to lift, followed by the opening of the drawbridge. Traffic
stopped on either side. A paddleboat slipped through the narrow channel, and I heard music. Passengers on the upper deck,
with drinks in hand, looked down and waved. *Margaritas on
the Mississippi!* The boat slid by and faded into the south. The
drawbridge closed, the lift bridge descended, and the fisherman
returned to the shimmering side of the waters.

3

One Saturday morning in November, I joined a group of thirty,
mostly students, gathered in a circle beneath a cottonwood tree
on the bluffs above the Minnesota River. I had heard of Healing
Minnesota Stories and had contacted its director, the Reverend
Jim Bear Jacobs, a Mohican and a Christian pastor who uses
stories and conversations to work for reconciliation and cultural
healing. Jim Bear welcomed me to join this group. With him
was Bob Klanderud, a Dakota elder who was burning white sage
in a sacred shell and directing the smoke with an eagle wing. Jim
Bear and Bob introduced themselves and offered thanks to the
four directions. As Jim Bear began to speak, Bob walked around
the circle, showing us how to draw the smoke over our heads in
blessing. Jim Bear explained the ritual's symbols.

"The shell comes from ocean depths; the eagle wing from the sky above. This smoke that surrounds us, then, joins our prayers with all creation, and blesses all that is between earth and sky."

Nearby stood St. Peter's Church, the oldest church in Minnesota; and to the north, across the river valley, the solid walls of old Fort Snelling. The walls of both the church and the fort were built of limestone quarried from the river bluffs.

Jim Bear told the story of creation in a way that seemed familiar and fantastic. He told of the Creator taking mud, making two-leggeds and setting them here, in this place. Jim Bear likened his story to the creation story from Hebraic tradition. "This," he said, "is our Garden of Eden. Here is where light first broke above the bluffs. Here is where birdsong first was heard. Here is where humans were pulled from the soil and first pressed their feet into the earth."

Then Jim Bear drew some darker threads into the fabric of his story—threads first spun in 1803 with the Louisiana Purchase, and then more tightly in the autumn of 1805, when Zebulon Pike arrived at this confluence and negotiated land away from the Dakota for what would become Fort Snelling. Where the fort now stands, Jim Bear told us, was declared to be the point of western demarcation. Settlers coming up the river would reach this point and be told they could settle to the east of here, but could not settle to the west of here. In reality, however, that did not happen, Jim Bear explained. The United States never did intend to honor that demarcation; but it was one of many things that was said.

As for the nearby church, built in 1853, Jim Bear said he holds no ill will toward the church. "I'm an ordained minister, after all. But we cannot ignore its presence either," he continued. "Like the fort, the church has been a force of domination. But it has begun to own its dark history, too, and is reaching out with genuine efforts of reconciliation."

Jim Bear's words were firm, clear, and unhurried; his voice was gentle. High above us, an eagle turned and rode an air current toward the east. We felt that we could sit all day beneath this tree and listen. But Jim Bear meant to take us to another site— and there, he told us, we would be sitting for quite some time.

We broke the circle, almost in silence, and formed a caravan of cars. Jim Bear led us from the parking lot, across the Mendota Bridge and down into the valley of the Fort Snelling State Park.

4

We gathered in a circle near the park's interpretive center. This time, we sat within an open structure made of stone and upward-thrusting timbers that leaned inward and surrounded a firepit. A nearby sign proclaimed, WOKIKSUYE K'A WOYUONIHAN, which means, "Remembering and honoring." We knew we were on sacred ground. The walls of Fort Snelling rose high on the bluff above us. Trails led into the woods to the east, to Bdote.

Jim Bear stood in silence. Several were distributing blankets to those who wanted them. The air had grown quite chilly and damp. The trees were bare, and the sky was leaden. We drew together tightly and settled in. Bob blessed Jim Bear with the eagle wing, dipping the wing into the smoke and touching it lightly to Jim Bear's head, his shoulders, his back, his chest, and his arms, even as Jim Bear began to speak.

"Whenever the stories of history are told," Jim Bear said, "they usually are presented as linear tales. Linear stories have a way of distancing us from the reality—that happened then, and this is now. But for indigenous peoples, stories do not exist in time—they exist in space—here, in this place. They are layered. They breathe. They are alive.

"Notice what's happening to your body," he suggested, "even now as you sit here in this valley. It is cold here. You have a blanket around you. But already you can feel your body responding to the stories and the songs that have sunk into this earth and remain here. As you walked from your car to this gathering site, you walked over ground that humans have been walking on for thousands of years. Your footsteps followed theirs. Here, you might begin to hear with different ears, and sense with different senses.

"Let me tell you what this valley meant for the Dakota," Jim Bear continued. And he told of how Dakota women, about to give birth, would come from far away, walking for days so that their children would be born here, in this valley of creation; so that their first breath would be drawn where humans first took breath; so that the very first birdsongs heard by their newborn would be where birdsong first was heard; so that the light that first broke across their vision would be in the valley where sun first broke across the bluffs and filled this valley with light. How very significant and sacred was this space!

"Now," he said, pausing poignantly, "how is it that this place of genesis came to be a place of genocide? You are sitting on the site of the first concentration camp in this land."

We sat in silence, stunned. I thought I knew about Fort Snelling; but never had I considered this place as paradox, as both a place of genesis and genocide. I felt a dark holiness descending.

And then the power of a living, breathing story encompassed us. Jim Bear's voice told us of the past, but a past that seemed so very present. He told us much of what we thought we knew, but in a way we did not know. He reminded us how a territory became a state, of what had been required for Minnesota, in 1857, to acquire statehood—substantial land (and hence the need for treaties), and a significant number of white male settlers.

We heard of the $1.6 million agreed upon for thirty-six million acres, and the story of the betrayals—of how, when the signers came to sign the treaty, they were forced to sign *two* documents. Most could not read. Most did not know that with the second document, they would sign away all the first document had promised. And then we heard of how—when the treaty came to Washington for ratification—the powers in Washington discovered that the land to be granted to the Dakota was the very fertile Minnesota valley.

"Have you not grown up with the Jolly Green Giant?" Jim Bear asked this group of young Minnesotans. "Have you not eaten the Jolly Green Giant's vegetables? This was the valley of the Jolly Green Giant!

"Not wishing to negotiate a new treaty," he continued, "the government officials simply drew new lines on the map to exclude the Dakota from the land of the green giant."

We heard of the drought that followed this betrayal, of years of starvation and suffering, and of hardened hearts. We heard of how, in Meeker County, an argument over stolen eggs and a killing of five settlers erupted into war in the late summer of 1862. We heard how Governor Ramsey said the Dakota "must be exterminated or driven forever beyond the borders of the state."

Jim Bear did not recount the battles of that summer, but lingered over two events that followed—the forced removal of the Dakota from the Minnesota River valley, and the trial and execution of thirty-eight Dakota warriors in Mankato.

"It was about this time of year," Jim Bear said, "when Dakota men, women, and children were brought here and confined in what we now would call a concentration camp." And as Jim Bear described conditions along the river that winter of 1862/63, we imagined the cold, the hunger, the despair and endless crying. Several hundred, he told us, never made it out.

"And then, December 26, the day after it celebrated the birth of the Prince of Peace," Jim Bear said softly, "the United States hung thirty-eight Dakota men in Mankato—all at once—the largest mass execution in the nation's history."

Then Jim Bear talked with us about forgiveness. "We must forgive the unforgivable," he said, "or we will destroy ourselves. But that does not mean we should forget." We had come there to remember, but were also there for healing.

Each listener was given a small amount of tobacco to hold in our hands. Jim Bear encouraged us to walk around this sacred space, reflecting silently or talking as we wished, then to place tobacco where we thought appropriate, as an offering, or prayer, or tribute. Here and there, among the leaves and trees were ribbons—prayer flags—fastened to stakes and tied to branches. We drifted into the woods. Some dropped pinches of tobacco here and there; others flung it all at once into the air. Some knelt and placed it reverently on the leaf-strewn ground.

5

The sun was dropping behind the trees when Jim Bear led us out and up to a third, sacred site above the confluence of the rivers—Oȟéyawahe, "the hill much visited." It's also known as Pilot

Knob, having served as a navigation point to steamboat pilots. But the hill is barely a hill now and scarcely visible from the river, for much of it long ago was scraped away for fill dirt. Here the Dakota had erected burial scaffolds for their dead, leaving the bodies aboveground for a season to serve the birds, rodents, and insects. Once a body had been reduced to bones, the hill would be revisited and the bones would be buried.

We were standing on a dead-end road, looking west across a field as Jim Bear spoke to us. Beyond the river stands Fort Snelling. Jim Bear asked us to imagine the hill rising up before us, bristling with scaffolds that hold the bodies of the dead. We thought of bodies, returning to nature, and the community of the living visiting their dead.

"Now consider that burial ground," Jim Bear said, pointing south toward Acacia Park Cemetery, which holds the bones of some notable Nordic Minnesotans. "No one would dare to skim an inch from that land. Can you imagine the outcry if someone sought to move the bones that are buried there? Yet the sacred ground of Oȟéyawahe was used as fill dirt, and unearthed bones were cast into a shed."

Jim Bear taught us even more about systemic forces when he explained how Oȟéyawahe had only recently been spared from being completely obliterated. This sacred land had been platted for luxury condominiums, and only the economic recession of 2008 prevented that from happening.

The sun had set, and Jim Bear concluded our day with words of benediction and a song of blessing, accompanied by the beating of the drum. Then he shook hands with each as we parted. "Tell your story," he said. "You are stories. You are stories wrapped in bodies."

6

On Cathedral Hill, adjacent to the Cathedral of Saint Paul and just south of Capitol Hill, stands the Minnesota History Center. It's a glorious structure, built of granite and glass, terra-cotta and copper. I walk from the Green Line Tenth Street Station, across the freeway, roaring with the morning rush hour, and ascend a long flight of stone steps that lead to the building. The great bronze doors yield readily, and I enter its corridors.

Here the stories of Minnesota are housed and celebrated—stories of who we were, and are, and yearn to be. Vast galleries of interactive exhibits make these stories accessible—splendid portrayals of our being in time. Most are devoted to particular themes—a specific generation, an immigrant group, or a story of working lives. This morning, the vaulted atrium and expansive hallways resound with exuberant voices of children on field trips.

I head up the grand staircase to the second floor and back to the secluded space of the Gale Family Library. Coats, bags, and pens are not allowed, so I take in only my laptop and a notebook, and join an eclectic group of scholars at wooden tables spread throughout the library. Some sit waiting for archival material to be brought up from the vaults. Some are scrutinizing photos or old maps, or scrolling through genealogical records. It's exhilarating to be with others immersed in the study of Minnesota's past.

The stories of Jim Bear Jacobs had awakened in me a desire for more—for more stories of our origins and of the sacredness of place. In time, this study would become a way for me to understand my own story in a fuller sense.

Among the history center's many books, I found the story of Philander Prescott and Naginowenah. It is, in many ways, a common tale of that time and place—white man marries indigenous woman, as told by the white man, not by the indigenous woman. I would have liked to hear Naginowenah's story. But as the name Prescott is what led me to this narrative, I perused *The Recollections of Philander Prescott*—guardedly, at first, then increasingly receptive as I was caught by its clarity, humility, and quiet sense of mystery.

Phil Prescott's story unfolded as Fort Snelling was being built. It was 1820. Phil was working in the sutler's store where Naginowenah, then eighteen, came frequently to trade. "Her appearance and conduct attracted my attention," Phil recalled. Several years passed before he determined to marry her, "after the Indian manner," as he put it; "so I took ten blankets, one gun, and five gallons of whiskey and a horse and went to the old chief's lodge." The chief accepted his proposal, but Naginowenah was reluctant and "did not like the idea of marrying," said Phil.

"At last, through much entreaty of the parents, she came for to be my wife or companion as long as I chose to live with her. Little did I think at that time I should live with her until old age. We passed the winter very comfortably together. The old chief lived in his tent near us all winter. I fed and clothed them all winter."

Years passed and children came—there would be nine. Phil took on various jobs and often was away from home. And then, it seems, in the winter of 1835/36, the death of two children brought on a spiritual crisis and conversion. Phil Prescott wrote:

"The two deaths, so close one upon the other, made me reflect seriously. The longer I went the more I thought on the subject and commenced praying. And I went and finally made up my mind to join the church, and I found no peace until I did make up my mind to do something."

He joined the Presbyterian Church near Lake Harriet on June 18, 1837. Philander then considered that it might be good to remarry Naginowenah in the church that he had joined. At the wedding, the Reverend Samuel Pond officiated, the same who, with his brother, Gideon Pond, created the Pond-Dakota alphabet that still is used today to write the Dakota language.

Zachariah, Phil's brother, ridiculed Phil's conversion, telling him he'd sold himself "for a pew in Heaven." But Phil held firm. "I stuck to the work of prayer, and believe I never shall be sorry for the step I took in joining the church. Repentance and faith had got [a] fast hold upon me, and I was determined to live by it. I never have seen the time yet but what I could say I wanted more of the love of God."

The year 1837 was a turning point—not only for Phil Prescott's spiritual life but for the life of the nations of North America. Across the land, there was a kind of desperation in the air. The financial panic of 1837 swept through Wall Street and beyond, closing businesses and banks and producing record unemployment. In the east, the movement for the abolition of slavery was gathering momentum.

For indigenous people near the river, 1837 marked a year of dispossession. The Winnebago (Ho-Chunk) were forced to sign a treaty late that year, forever displacing them from their lands. In the summer of 1837, the Chippewa (Ojibwe) ceded timber lands along the Saint Croix; and in September, the Dakota ceded lands east of the Mississippi. "By such cessions," notes historian Dorothy Ahlgren, "the US obtains possession of the triangle between the Mississippi and St. Croix rivers, as well as a part of northern Wisconsin." It was at the vertex of that triangle where Phil Prescott built a house and established the town of Prescott.

Winter passed and spring returned before I returned to Prescott. I crossed the bridge, rounded the corner past the clock tower, and parked on Broad Street, near the Muddy Waters Bar and Grill above the confluence. I was thinking about the polarization of our country—prompted, no doubt, by simply crossing from Minnesota to Wisconsin and considering the political divisions of these two states. I thought of Philander and Naginowenah, and the troubled and deeply polarized times in which they lived.

Prescott had not set out to build this town; he simply responded to a call when it came:

> Towards Spring [1839] I had one offer from the officers of the fort to go down to the St. Croix and take charge of a claim they had taken up for a town site. They agreed to furnish me with one thousand dollars to build a house and store with, and give me one-eighth of all the land and buildings. I had nothing to do, so I accepted their offer and went to work.

That same summer, a large group of Ojibwe—about a thousand men, women, and children—came down to feast and council with the Dakota. Then, somewhere out near Bde Maka Ska, a skirmish broke out between the two groups that grew into an armed conflict. Hostilities continued along the Mississippi and Saint Croix Rivers. But as for Prescott, "I went on to work and finished my house at the mouth of the Saint Croix. There was no business then at that point."

I've been thinking, almost constantly, on the racial violence of my time, erupting in the summer of 2020 in nearly the same place in Minneapolis, not far from Bde Maka Ska. It has forced a necessary awakening to the tenacity of systemic racism—in the Twin Cities and across the nation. The example of Phil Prescott, nearly two centuries ago, has increased my desire to live with integrity in a world profoundly unjust. At the turbulent confluence of cultures, he did his work—building a house, becoming fluent in Dakota, practicing fairness in trade, and in translation as a government interpreter. And then, there was always his work of maintaining a vital relationship with Naginowenah.

Of Naginowenah, we know much less. Together, she and Philander had nine children, and welcomed many friends and strangers to their home. Historian Jane Lamm Carroll described the wedding of their daughter Lucy on New Year's Day of 1850 as "the highlight of the Fort Snelling social season."

But their family struggled with enormous cultural challenges, as Carroll explains, especially in deciding how to raise and educate their biracial children in a world where only white lives mattered. Naginowenah experienced these tensions keenly as her children became more anglicized. "Her life straddled both Indian and Euro-American cultures," says Carroll, "but her identity was as a Dakota woman."

Philander was among the first to be killed when the Dakota war broke out in the late summer of 1862. The manner of his death has gripped me. At that time, Philander and Naginowenah were living at the Lower Sioux Agency, a hundred miles west of Minneapolis. It has been a pattern all too familiar in this country's history—systemic racism erupting into violence. When it happened that summer of 1862, Philander tried to flee for safety

along the Minnesota River. John H. Stevens, an early settler and
Minnesota legislator and a familiar guest in the home of Philander and Naginowenah, relates the story of his death.

> Mr. Prescott had gone several miles along the west bank of the
> Minnesota river when he was overtaken, his murderers came
> and talked with him. He reasoned with them, saying: "I am an
> old man; I have lived with you now forty-five years, almost half
> a century. My wife and children are among you, of your own
> blood; I have never done you any harm, and have been your
> true friend in all your troubles; why should you wish to kill
> me?" Their reply was: "We would save your life if we could, but
> the WHITE MAN MUST DIE; we cannot spare your life; our orders
> are to kill all white men; we cannot spare you." It is said upon
> the authority of the Indians that he was shot while talking with
> them and looking calmly into their eyes.

Somehow, the flows of history catch us all by surprise.
Their fluencies—whether of affluence, or of effluence, or of
influence—carry us ceaselessly toward confluence. The waters
and all they carry with them will come together. And there will
be blood.

What is it like to watch the small stream of your life empty
out into a larger and more powerful flow of events? What is it
like for a young black man today to feel his life being pressed out
by the knee of a policeman while he cries out, "I can't breathe!"?
What is it like to be an old white man and be shot, looking
calmly into the eyes of those who can no longer spare you? And
for those who live on, what is it like to know these individual
lives as sacrifice to something vaster and more urgent? These are
not opposing streams; they are moving toward convergence.

And what new and larger stream emerges from all the turbulence, carrying us on toward other meetings and other mergings?

7

More than 250 rivers flow into the Mississippi, draining 40 percent or more of the Lower 48. Some confluences are turbulent,
like the muddy Missouri flowing in from the west. Others, like
the great Ohio, flowing in from the east, merge more calmly. It's
a pattern that geoscientist Ellen Wohl, who specializes in rivers,
has noticed about the Mississippi River basin: "From the western
half of the basin comes the sediment that keeps the river a turbid
brown. From the northern and eastern portions comes the water."

Confluences matter ecologically. Stephen Rice, a British river
scientist, says confluences provide sites of high biological pro-
ductivity and habitat variability, as well as creating deep pools of
critical refuge for mobile species—for breeding, for protection
from predators, and as shelter from warming temperatures or
winter's freeze.

In his book *River Confluences, Tributaries and the Fluvial
Network*, Rice and his colleagues describe five basic morpho-
logical features created by a confluence: (1) a scour hole; (2)
a tributary-mouth bar that slopes into the scour hole; (3) a
mid-channel bar or bars within the post-confluence channel; (4)
bank-attached lateral bars; and (5) a region of sediment accumulation near the upstream confluence corner, perhaps associated
with flow stagnation. "Confluences can seem unruly places,"
he says, "their morphologies complex, even untidy, frequently
unstable and shifting."

Such topographical features might serve as metaphorical cautions, too, as we negotiate the current confluences of human lives and cultures. Knowing a confluence produces scouring, accumulation of sediment, instability in the channel, and other unpredictable barriers, engineers find it prudent to locate bridges above or below the confluence, rather than directly across the confluence itself. So, too, in building bridges for our society, we might draw social wisdom from the physical structures we have engineered.

A hundred miles downstream from Prescott, three rivers join the Mississippi. The clear waters of the Black and La Crosse Rivers enter from Wisconsin; from Minnesota, a bit farther downstream, the silt-laden waters of the Root. The Root River, unlike the Black and La Crosse, runs mostly through tilled farmland, bringing in a great load of sediment. A lush delta spreads out from this extraordinary confluence, creating intricate patterns of channels, inlets, and islands. It's a recreational paradise, as well as an ideal research site for the University of Wisconsin's River Studies Center, where faculty and students investigate problems of watersheds and wetlands, invasive species, hydrological development, fluvial dynamics, and the effects of toxicity on aquatic communities. Upstream from the confluence, behind Lock and Dam No. 7, spreads Lake Onalaska, the widest point on the Mississippi.

8

Spring break came late and promised warmth enough for camping. I determined to get myself back to the Great River Road for a short excursion.

I strapped a borrowed kayak to my car, packed a tent and camping gear, and set out again for Prescott and the road beyond. I envisioned a slow, reflective trip, stopping in cafés and shops along the way, pausing at riverfronts and overlooks. Many shops and sites remained closed from winter.

Driving was delightful, passing through one river town after another, feeling the car rising and falling with the road. I passed prosperous dairy farms and tree farms. Along the river's edge, the trees were just beginning to leaf, not yet shrouding the topography and rocks, the low-lying sloughs, and the reassuring glimpses of the river itself. I passed Diamond Bluff, passed Bay City, passed the lovely Lake Pepin overlook, Maiden Rock, the tiny towns of Pepin and Stockholm, the long stretch of Nelson bottoms, and stopped at Alma, a two-street town, the parallel upper and lower streets connected by stairs. The towns flow together in memory—Genoa, with a kind of old-world charm, bluffs rising behind the village, Victory, De Soto, Ferryville—and a long, winding stretch to Prairie du Chien, narrow lanes hugging the bluffs, and breathtaking views!

South of Prairie du Chien, where the Wisconsin River meets the Mississippi, stretches an interlacing region of waters and wetlands, forests, islands, sloughs, and bottomlands—part of the vast Upper Mississippi River National Wildlife and Fish Refuge. On the Iowa side of the river, opposite the confluence, rise the bluffs of Pikes Peak State Park and, a bit farther north, the Effigy Mounds National Monument. At the confluence itself is Wyalusing State Park, bounded on the north by the Wisconsin River and on the west by the Mississippi. It's a paradise for anyone who loves wild things.

At Wyalusing, I pitched my tent on a high ridge overlooking the Wisconsin River. From this height, you can see the shimmering, islanded river below, stretching its long, jeweled fingers toward the Mississippi River. The campground was nearly deserted. I set up my tent; a good strong breeze encouraged me to stake it down tightly. Then I drove down from the ridge to the boat landing below.

I'm not much of a kayaker; I really prefer to canoe with a partner. But needing some adventure, I soon was paddling through the narrow, calm backwaters, following the blue diamond signs that mark the canoe trail. You can follow this lovely, watery trail north and west for several miles to where it meets the Mississippi River. Then, if you wish, you can paddle down the Mississippi River, hugging the eastern shore until you reach the southern end of the canoe trail, and return up the trail to the landing. I chose not to kayak the complete loop, but settled for meandering among the backwaters.

When I returned to the campground that afternoon, I was dismayed to see the campsite next to mine now occupied. "Empty sites all along the ridge," I muttered to myself. "Why should anyone need to camp right here?" A white Subaru with Illinois plates was parked beside a small tent. "Land of Lincoln," I read. No one in sight. I set about preparing dinner, building a fire, then sinking into my camp chair with the book I had brought with me.

I don't know how long I'd been reading—the light was fading—when a shadow fell over my page and I looked up, startled. There stood a man, outlined against the orange glow of the sky, with hand outstretched. Two dark, shining bottles hung from his fingers.

"Too late to read now," he said pleasantly. "Join me for a beer?"

I accepted the outstretched beer; it was already uncapped. He extended his other hand. "I'm Jerome," he said. And he was right, it was too late to read. I stood, let my book fall to the ground, and gestured toward the picnic table. Rarely had I met an African American on a campground, and so I welcomed this opportunity. "Cheers."

We sat, each straddling a bench on opposite sides of the picnic table. There was that awkward silence that often follows first encounters—somewhat magnified, for me, by race and age. I guessed he must be younger by some twenty years or more. We sipped our beers and gazed out toward the western bluffs. The sun was going down.

Jerome asked about my kayak, and I described my afternoon's adventure on the waters.

"First time I've seen the Mississippi," he said softly.

"You're from Chicago?" I guessed. "What brought you way out here . . . to see the Mississippi?"

Jerome was headed for the delta, he said, to hear some delta blues. I assumed he meant New Orleans, but he corrected me. "No, not New Orleans. Clarksdale, Mississippi. The Delta Blues Museum. Home of Muddy Waters." And so it was we talked of music and migration—foregoing all the usual pleasantries of conversation—jobs, sports, families.

He told me of his love of Muddy Waters, who moved up north in the 1940s from Mississippi to Chicago and helped develop the Chicago blues. He explained what made the Delta blues so different from the urban blues of Chicago and New York, and talked of other greats like Willie Dixon and Luther Allison, though it became for me a humbling tutorial.

"You must know Willie Dixon," he asked at one point.

"No, can't say I do," I said.

"Oh, man! 'Hoochie Coochie Man'? 'Little Red Rooster'? 'I Just Want to Make Love to You'?"

"Uh, wasn't that the Rolling Stones?" I grasped to say something knowledgeable.

"Well, yeah. All those white guys sang Dixon's songs—Led Zeppelin, the Doors, Eric Clapton, Grateful Dead, Van Morrison . . ." How did I not know this?

Jerome told me when the Beatles came to the United States in 1964, they wanted, most of all, to see Muddy Waters. A reporter asked them, "Where is that?" And one of the Beatles replied incredulously, "Man, don't you know your own history?" We laughed. "Course, I wasn't even born then," Jerome said, "but that's the story I heard," and we laughed again.

Jerome said he started listening to blues at an early age. He had an aunt who sang the blues, and now he played piano with a jazz band. "But it was always about the singing," he said. "The blues—just singing about life, you know—'got up this morning,' or 'sun goin' down this evening,' and somebody gone and left." He lifted his cap and rubbed his head vigorously, staring at the fire.

"But not many people of color into blues now," Jerome said, "especially my age and younger. I once heard B. B. King say, 'I look out my audience, and all I see is white folks. Glad you're here,' he say, 'but when I die, the blues die with me.' Well, B. B. King dead now. And the blues . . . ?" His voice trailed away.

It was much later, long after Jerome went back to his site, that a mighty storm sprang up and shook the tent, pulling at the tent stakes and snapping the rain fly. The sounds of thunder exhilarated me, but I worried that the wind might carry me, with the tent, over the precipice. I abandoned my tent and soon fell asleep to the sound of the rain against the roof of my car.

When I woke in the morning, Jerome had gone. The campsite was empty. I made some coffee and set out walking along the ridge. I was eager to get back on the road, but the tent needed drying, and it was a bright, clear morning. Several turkey vultures were circling the valley below, their fingered wings stretched wide.

A short way down the ridge, I found an overlook with a monument of stone, commemorating the extinction of passenger pigeons. I read:

DEDICATED TO THE LAST PASSENGER PIGEON
Shot at Babcock, Sept. 1899
This Species Became Extinct Through the Avarice and
Thoughtlessness of Man

Another sign explained how what was once the most populous bird in North America went "from billions to none." John Muir, who grew up on the Fox River, not far from there, recalled passenger pigeons streaming from horizon to horizon, "like a mighty river in the sky, widening, contracting, descending like falls and cataracts, and rising suddenly here and there in huge ragged masses like high-plashing spray."

When this Wyalusing monument was dedicated in 1947, Aldo Leopold, another Wisconsin conservationist, said, "It symbolizes our sorrow. We grieve because no [one] will see again the onrushing phalanx of victorious birds, sweeping a path for spring across the March skies." He also said, "For one species to mourn the death of another is a new thing under the sun."

Now it's not a new thing under the sun. The streams of human life have grown torrential, displacing and consuming other streams of birds, amphibians, butterflies and bees, things that move and things that flower. An extinction crisis is before us; as I write these words, a pandemic rages. This confluence is a fitting place to mourn, to think about the diminishment of all living things, including the impoverishment of human life. And yet . . .

And yet, the thing is, the fluence persists, the fluency of life carries on. Affluence, influence, confluence. Birds stream through Wyalusing on the great North American flyway. And the silver carp, too, and bighead and grass carp, and zebra mussels— invasives all. Streams of people, too, still migrate up and down the river—like Muddy Waters coming up from Mississippi, or Jerome on his pilgrimage down to the delta, mourning the loss of the blues and wanting to connect with its more primal origins.

I left Wyalusing knowing that I, too, am mourning, yet still reaching. And what I most remember from my time at Wyalusing is the image of Jerome at sundown, with outstretched fingers, offering me a beer and conversation.

9

Langston Hughes was seventeen, traveling by train to Mexico to see his father, when his train crossed over the Eads Bridge of Saint Louis at sunset. The golden glow on the muddy waters inspired Hughes to write a poem that launched a wonderful, poetic career. The poem ends with these words:

> I heard the singing of the Mississippi when Abe Lincoln
> went down to New Orleans, and I've seen its muddy
> bosom turn all golden in the sunset.
> I've known rivers:
> Ancient, dusky rivers.
> My soul has grown deep like the rivers.

There's a magic to the rivers running through Saint Louis. Like the "ancient, dusky rivers" of Hughes's poem—the Euphrates, the Congo, and the Nile—something about the rivers around Saint Louis speaks to the soul. Here the Illinois River from the east, and the Missouri River from the west, join the Mississippi at its heart.

T. S. Eliot, who grew up here, said, "St. Louis affected me more deeply than any other environment has ever done. I feel that there is something in having passed one's childhood beside the big river, which is incommunicable to those people who have not." He called the Mississippi River a "strong, brown god." Asked to write an introduction for a 1950 edition of *The Adventures of Huckleberry Finn*, Eliot said Mark Twain was "a native that accepts the River God," and consequently, Eliot believed, Twain wrote "a much greater book than he could have known he was writing."

Kate Chopin, born and buried in Saint Louis, is best remembered for her novel *The Awakening*, set on the Louisiana Gulf Coast one summer in the 1890s. It's about the sensual and spiritual awakening of a twenty-eight-year-old woman named Edna, for whom "the voice of the sea is seductive, never ceasing, whispering, clamoring, murmuring, inviting the soul to wander for a spell in abysses of solitude; to lose itself in mazes of inward contemplation." A few years before *The Awakening*, Chopin wrote a story for *Vogue*, imagining a man at the center of the Eads Bridge, looking down at "the deep, broad, swift, black river," lost in a maze of contemplation as vast as Edna's:

> The wind was blowing fiercely and keenly. The darkness where
> he stood was impenetrable. The thousands of lights in the city

he had left seemed like all the stars of heaven massed together, sinking into some distant mysterious horizon, leaving him alone in a black, boundless universe.

I had come to Saint Louis for a literary conference. It was autumn, and as I was on a sabbatical, I came early by a week or so. I'd seen the tourist sites before; now I wanted to spend time by the river before sitting in hotel meeting rooms and listening to academic papers.

Pere Marquette State Park is gorgeous—eight thousand acres of wooded hills, trails, and ravines near the confluence of the Illinois and Mississippi Rivers—named for a Jesuit missionary explorer, Jacques Marquette, who stopped here in 1673 with his cartographer, Louis Jolliet, and their company of voyageurs.

By some roguish coincidence, a Catholic missionary befriended me upon my arrival! The park was full that autumn afternoon—no vacancies in the expansive lodge, or the cabins, or any of the drive-in campsites. But there was an open tenting area, I was told. So I located an unclaimed grassy spot and parked my car. Sheltered by a hill on one side, with a valley on the other, the site seemed ideal. Halfway up the hillside, an Osage orange tree was dropping hedge apples; I would hear the thudding of these softball-size fruits hitting the ground throughout the night!

I had just begun to raise my tent when Charles D—, a nearby camper, came bicycling by and offered to give me a hand. Now, I am quite capable of setting up my tent, but Charles seemed so cheerful, I accepted his assistance.

Charles travels the country in an old van, filled with books and Bibles and symbols of his Catholic faith. He earns an adequate living as a wildlife photographer, he said, but his real mission was volunteering wherever needed, and he was on his way to the Gulf Coast to help with hurricane relief.

"Living Franciscan-like," I observed.

"I guess I do maintain a look of poverty," he said, self-consciously, "but I'm no priest." He did, however, invite me to Mass the following morning.

At six o'clock, I was awakened by a voice outside my tent. "Thomas. Coffee here. On the table." I crawled from my sleeping bag and unzipped the door. Charles had gone, but a thermos stood on the picnic table. By seven, we were on our way to St. Patrick Church in Grafton.

On the way to Grafton, Charles suggested that we stop to see a monument, a cross, commemorating Marquette's arrival in Illinois. The monument, built in 1929, stands beside the highway, overlooking the Illinois River. We climbed some stairs to an alcove behind the cross. "At this place in early August 1673 Marquette, Jolliet and five companions entered Illinois, dawn-heralds of Religion, Civil Government and Consecrated Labor." Charles took pictures while I fretted over "dawn-heralds of religion, civil government and consecrated labor."

Charles seemed to know all about that journey of Marquette—their paddling down the Fox and Wisconsin Rivers to the Mississippi, then going on down the Mississippi as far as the Arkansas River where they stopped. When Marquette got back to this very place, he chose to go up the Illinois River to Lake Michigan, rather than returning the way he had come.

St. Patrick Church in Grafton is a simple structure, built more than a century ago of limestone quarried from the nearby bluffs. The interior is plain, almost like a rural Baptist church, but for the statues and the ornate altar. There was neither choir nor organ, but Charles sang out lustily, without the book. As for me, I struggled to follow him in the liturgy. Not being Catholic, I could not take Communion. My attention wandered during the homily and sacrament. I gazed at the statues of the Holy Family, pondered the stations of the cross, and studied the blue stained glass above the altar depicting Father Marquette kneeling in a canoe.

"Would you like to see Our Lady of the Rivers?" Charles asked when the service had concluded. "It's just across the river." Unfortunately, the ferry to "just across the river" was not running, so we drove some twenty miles east and crossed the beautiful, cabled Clark Bridge in Alton. Then we tracked back on the other side to the little town of Portage Des Sioux, where a tall white shrine had been built, in gratitude, after the devastating flood of 1993. Now, the river was again running high, so we had no access to the shrine itself. We gazed in silence at the still white form.

On our drive back, I talked with Charles about my curiosity of confluences and my wish to discover something of mystery or sacredness. While Charles expressed a deep, religious sensibility, he seemed unable to respond to a mystical sense of things.

Yet we both enjoyed our conversation and perhaps were a bit reluctant to part ways. When we got back to Pere Marquette, Charles offered to show me some overlooks and sites that had delighted him. Near the base of one large oak, he pointed out some overlapping fungi among the leaves. "Hen of the woods," he said.

"Are they edible?" I asked.

"Well, you know what we say—all mushrooms are edible, but some you only eat once!" He laughed. "But these are quite edible. Need to cook them a bit."

We continued walking, and Charles asked, "Have you heard the story about Jesus and the mushrooms?" He looked at me with a childlike glee.

"No, I can't say that I have." I braced myself for a corny joke; but instead, he told a story that seemed like some faraway folktale.

One day, Jesus and Peter were walking through a village when they came upon a wedding party. As they passed, the father of the bride called out for them to join. And Jesus, who loved to be at weddings, warned Peter that these were poor people; therefore, they should eat no cake, but only bread. Then Jesus and Peter joined the party. But Peter, when no one was looking, took some of the cake and hid it in a pouch beneath his robe. As the party progressed, Peter took more of the cake, and added it to his pouch until the pouch was full.

After a while, they continued on their way. But Peter would hang back to nibble on the cake. And each time Peter took a bite, Jesus, who seemed to have eyes in the back of his head, asked, "What are you eating?"

Peter would spit out the cake and say, "Nothing," and make up some excuse for his lagging. This happened over and over until all the cake was gone. Then Jesus turned to Peter and said, "You've eaten the cake I told you not to eat, and you have also lied to me. Now, go back and pick up every piece that you have spit out."

Jesus waited for a very long time. When Peter returned, he said, "I did not find any cake. But wherever I spat, I found this." He handed Jesus a pouch full of white growths.

Jesus said, "This is what grew from the food that you spat." Then Peter wept and told Jesus he was sorry, and Jesus forgave him. So they both went on until they came to a cottage where a poor woman lived. Jesus gave her Peter's pouch and told her to cook what was in it. They turned out to be mushrooms; and the woman cooked them with seasoning and salt so that they were very good.

"So it is," said Charles, "that mushrooms became food for the poor, and poor people have learned how to find them. But to Peter, he said, 'Because you remain hungry, mushrooms will never fill you up.'"

"There you have it," I said, not knowing what else to say.

Charles beamed.

We parted soon after, and I've not seen him since. But this European folktale teases me yet with its understated lesson.

In the late afternoon, I drove back to Grafton to the Loading Dock, a restaurant on the edge of the Mississippi River, right at the mouth of the Illinois River. One online posting read: "Grafton rocks! Nowhere else quite like it. It's like a custom car and motor-cycle theme park. Good food, good people, good live bands."

The sunshine was bright, the river brisk and dazzling, and the dockside tables were ready, though the yellow umbrellas had not been unfurled. It was like sitting on the deck of a great ship, about to set sail. Here, the confluence is wide. Several large islands split the Mississippi into four or five channels, creating an expansive feeling, as if several streams are converging here, not just the two.

"I want to spend some time at the confluence," I told the barkeeper when she asked.

"You've come to the right place," she said. "Spend as much time here as you'd like. There'll be music starting soon." She suggested a rum river mystic; it was a perfect blend of spirits!

Grafton was nearly destroyed by the flood of 1993. Unlike other river towns, Grafton has no levee, and the historic flood poured in across the town. Journalist Barry Yeoman says, "The absence of a levee has turned Grafton into an experiment in how more natural river management might work." After the flood, the town cleared away the devastated buildings and opened the riverfront to recreation and to low-impact structures. "We let the river come in," Yeoman reports the mayor saying, "and we let the river go out."

I sipped my rum river mystic and thought on these two ways of living with the river—across the way, the shrine to Our Lady of the Rivers, signifying prayer as gratitude and supplication; and here, the dockside, representing openness to whatever the river brings. Both are understandable responses to the flood of 1993 and to floods yet to come. But I wonder. Are these conflicting or complementary ways—ritual and receptivity? Both seem essential for whatever might be called sacred.

By the time I'd composed several pages of notes, the band was set up. Two men and a woman, almost as old as I am, were soon belting out oldies from decades past: *Rollin', rollin', rollin' on the river* . . . I listened long, and then I left and wandered to a nearby winery. I saw one label I knew I simply had to try—Confluence Conundrum.

10

So many! I thought. I must have spoken my thoughts aloud. I was looking at the checklist of nearly three hundred species of migrating birds at the Riverlands Migratory Bird Sanctuary.

"Exciting, huh?" the volunteer replied. But she was gazing at a group of adolescents, in constant motion, who were standing by the wall of windows. "It's the trumpeter swans," she said. Then she turned toward me.

"The swans arrived earlier than we expected, but perfect timing for these kids. They came up from Saint Louis," she continued. "And when they got here, these kids—most of them—were looking at their phones. Then, one spotted the swan, and that's all it took! Look," she said. "No one is on their phone."

Riverlands, I learned, was made possible through a remarkable collaboration of the Audubon Society with the US Army Corps of Engineers, just north of the Great Rivers confluence. Here, more than a thousand acres of restored marshes and wet prairie provide sanctuary for migrating birds.

Nearly 40 percent of all the birds of North America use the Mississippi River flyway in their spring and fall migrations, and this sanctuary provides important stopover habitat and food resources. It's a birder's paradise; it can also be a doorway into wonder for those who never knew they hungered for the nourishment of natural beauty.

I spent the better part of the morning wandering the trails through fields and marshlands with my binoculars and field guide. By the muddy edges of a shallow pond, I came upon a solitary birder who asked if I had spotted a semipalmated plover. "Pretty rare, especially now," she said, "but I'm seeing lots of killdeers."

11

The Lewis and Clark Confluence Tower will put you high above the point where the Missouri meets the Mississippi. You might find a more thrilling vista a dozen miles south in the ancient city of Cahokia. There, you can climb the ascending levels of Monks Mound, the largest earthen pyramid in North America, and ponder the sprawling mystery of a vanished civilization on the edge of where the Mississippi River flowed a thousand years ago. At the Lewis and Clark Confluence Tower, however, an elevator whisks you to the top, stopping at 50, then 100, then 150 feet above the river.

I found the vista to be expansive—but elusive. Waters were nearing flood stage, and from the tower, I could see why, earlier in the day, it had been impossible for me to reach the confluence point, either by car or by foot, on the other side of the river.

On my way to the confluence tower, I'd stopped at the Melvin Price Locks and Dam, the next-to-last step on the staircase of dams descending the Mississippi. The river had swollen overnight, and all nine of the dam's Tainter gates were open wide. An engineer had led our small group to the top of the dam, and from its dizzying height, we looked straight down upon the swift-flowing river pouring through the gates and the largest of two locks. There was no barge traffic.

When Marquette passed this spot in 1673, the sound and sight astonished him. He recalled:

> Sailing quietly in clear and calm water, we heard the noise of a rapid, into which we were about to run. I have seen nothing more dreadful. An accumulation of larger and entire trees, branches, and floating islands, was issuing from the mouth of the river Pekistanouï [Missouri], with such impetuosity that we could not without great danger risk passing through it. So great was the agitation that the water was very muddy, and could not become clear.

I want to be astonished. Standing on the upper level of the tower, I tried to evoke some sense of wonder. While there are no dreadful rapids, there is a deep stillness. From this height, I could see the Mississippi flowing past, and the Missouri in the distance, pouring in, silently, from beyond the point. Here the waters of the west flowed toward me, joining the Mississippi River. Here come the waters from the lands of my youth—trickles seeping up from the Ogallala Aquifer beneath the high plains of eastern Wyoming, appearing as an intermittent stream near my home in southern Niobrara County, then becoming the Niobrara River, meandering past the sandhills of Nebraska, joining the Snake and Keya Paha Rivers, and eventually, the Missouri at the border with South Dakota. Here come the waters from the Frenchman Creek that flowed past the cottonwood trees where I played and fished and built a tree house as a child in southern Nebraska. Here come the waters from the Platte, and, of course, the Big Muddy itself, all the way from Montana, passing the bones of my mother on a hill in north Omaha—all this water, gathered together and carrying its great freight of memory.

But the sense of wonder did not come. It's a grand vista, but not awesome. No sense of transcendence or mystery. Perhaps I'm too old. Perhaps the ruthless human presence, visible all around the tower—the dam, the haze of Saint Louis, the freeways, the storage tanks, the industrial complexes—desacralized these rivers and their awesome confluence. Ever since Bdote, I've lamented how our history of exploration has been a history of exploitation.

Nevertheless, I went to the nearby Camp River Dubois, a reconstruction of the site where Lewis and Clark spent the winter of 1804/05 before they set out, up the Missouri River, to

explore the Louisiana Territory. No one actually knows precisely
where they wintered; the site is "probably underwater," I was
told, for the confluence itself has long since shifted. So, what I
experienced at Camp River Dubois was not a "real" historical
place but an effective inducement to imagine such a time and
a place.

A kindly docent from the visitor's center agreed to take me
on a private tour of the reconstructed camp. The tourist season had ended, most of the buildings were closed and all the
reenactors gone. She told me there was no certainty this reconstruction even looked like the original, although sketches from
Clark's field notes had guided the designers. The log palisades
and living quarters were built of white oak, selectively harvested
from a nearby forest, then notched and raised and chinked. She
led me into the barracks and the officers' quarters, and described
the camp experience of waiting—of the drilling and the drinking and the brawling that could break out on those long winter
nights. But mostly she talked of Captain Clark's success in bringing discipline and cohesion to this unruly, newly formed Corps
of Discovery.

When our tour had ended, I told the docent I'd like to linger.
"Oh, I understand," she said gently, which truly surprised me,
for I myself did not understand my own desire to linger. She said
she would return in a moment. I zipped my jacket and turned
up the collar and leaned against the log building, weathered and
gray. Bits of mud chinking were falling out in places.

There is no real history here, I kept thinking. *Nothing has
actually happened here. It's just a fabrication for the curious.* And
yet . . . And yet there was something tugging at me. Was it
merely the associations of memory—a spare, log fort within a

flat, open setting, evoking the barren high plains of my child-hood, and frontier places with actual coordinates? There must be more, something else given off.

The docent came back with a well-worn book. "Here," she said. "I'm not sure what you're looking for, but this might be of interest to you. Take your time. I'll be here awhile." It proved to be a book of brief reflections, letters, and descriptions of Camp River Dubois.

Twentysomething John Ordway had been a sergeant in the army and was eager for his adventure with Lewis and Clark. On the day before the corps departed Camp River Dubois, he wrote a letter to his parents, back home in New Hampshire:

Camp River Dubois April the 8th 1804

Honored Parence.

I now embrace this oppertunity of writeing to you once more to let you know where I am and where I am going. I am well thank God, and in high Spirits. I am now on an expidition to the westward, with Capt. Lewis and Capt. Clark, who are appointed by the Presidant of the United States to go on an expidition through the interior parts of North America. We are to ascend the Missouri River with a boat as far as it is navigable and then go by land, to the western ocean, if nothing prevents, &c. This party consists of 25 picked Men of the armey & country likewise and I am so happy as to be one of them pick'd from the armey, and I and all the party are if wee live to Return, to Receive our Dis-charge whenever we return again to the United States if we chuse it. This place is on the Mississippi River opisite to the mouth of the Missouri River and we are to start in ten days up the Missouri River. This has been our winter quarters. Wee expect to be gone 18 months or two years. Wee are to Receive a great Reward for this expidition, when wee Return. I am to Receive 15 dollars pr. month and at least 400 ackers of first Rate land, and if we make Great Discoveries as we expect, the United States has promised to make us Great Rewards more than we are promised.

Ordway journaled every day of the journey, calling attention to what he saw, until the day they arrived back in Saint Louis, "the party all considerable much rejoiced that we have the Expedition Completed."

Days later, at home in my library, I had to find out what happened to John Ordway. I learned he went home, married, and returned to the Mississippi River, settling downstream in New Madrid. There he prospered and soon had a thousand acres of "first rate land."

Then, during the winter of 1811/12, three earthquakes shook the region of New Madrid, and the Mississippi River ran backward! Ordway's property was ruined. Having chronicled a new world opening before him, he now watched the earth heave, the river run backward, and towns swept away. It must have felt like the end of the world. His family survived and lived on in New Madrid; but for Ordway, the world had changed, and in five or six years, he was dead.

I left Camp River Dubois before I understood the appeal of that outpost, or what it might mean. But some magic of the place had gripped me, nonetheless—like the exhilaration of a "thin place," where boundaries of time begin to blur, and memory mingles with expectancy. What was, and what yet may be, flood into what is.

I did understand, however, that the docent of Dubois, by placing that book in my hand, reminded me of my dependency on language—how time and place are fused by language, and narrative invests it with significance.

In the winter months that followed, I picked up the journals of Ordway, Lewis, and Clark, and noticed how often the mouth of a river marked the progress of their journey. I found their journaling to be not merely a log or record of accomplishment but the voicing of perceptions and emotions, descriptions of beauty, abundance, and "scenes of visionary enchantment," as Lewis once put it.

Exactly one year from leaving Camp River Dubois, the Corps of Discovery set out again from Fort Mandan, their second wintering site, in what is now North Dakota. Here, Sacagawea joined them. For Meriwether Lewis, this was the real beginning of their adventure. On April 7, 1805, with the barge and its crew returning to Saint Louis, Meriwether Lewis pondered the journey ahead—the remaining "little fleet" of six canoes and two pirogues upon which they would depend, his own feelings of anxiety for their safety and preservation, the two thousand miles ahead of unknown interior, and "the good or evil that it had in store for us." Then Lewis set down this poignant reflection:

> However, as the state of mind in which we are, generally gives the coloring to events, when the imagination is suffered to wander into futurity, the picture which now presented itself to me was a most pleasing one, entertaining as I do, the most confident hope of succeeding in a voyage which had formed a darling project of mine for the last ten years, I could but esteem this moment of my departure as among the most happy of my life.

It's a magical moment for Lewis, a threshold, "when the imagination is suffered to wander into futurity." Hope springs into being—hope of succeeding, and confidence that what he had dreamed of would be carried on to completion. In this moment of enchantment, Lewis looks at his crew and sees them all "in excellent health and spirits, zealously attached to the enterprise, and anxious to proceed; not a whisper of murmur or discontent to be heard among them, but all act in unison, and with the most perfect harmony."

Lingering for a time at Camp River Dubois began to stir me imaginatively to "wander into futurity," thinking not so much on what had happened as on what could happen. What would it be like to bring together, in winter, an unruly and diverse group of people, and to create enough order and cohesion for an arduous journey into the unknown?

I live in a nation deeply divided; and the contradictory currents of our time grow more divergent and unruly. Is confluence even possible? What would be needed to bring these powerful streams together? What new river might be imagined to carry us all into a satisfying futurity?

There have been polarized times in our nation's history, and leaders who practiced a kind of "confluence" thinking to generate new currents of vision. There was Abraham Lincoln through the American Civil War, and FDR through the decade of the Depression, when extreme ideologies of fascism and of communism were both gaining strength. In 1937, with "one-third of a nation ill-housed, ill-clad, ill-nourished," FDR articulated a vision that honored both its "old foundations" and its "new materials of social justice." "In our personal ambitions we are individualists," he said. "But in our seeking for economic and political progress as a nation, we all go up, or else we all go down, as one people."

Such connections did not come to me all at once at Camp River Dubois as I leaned against a log wall with a book in my hand. My thoughts then were more personal, mixing memories of childhood with anticipations of my future. But I think it was the first time I experienced, for myself, the sacredness of confluence. I resolved to consider what it might mean for me to place myself intentionally where streams come together.

12

Months passed before I finally got to Cairo, where the Mississippi meets the Ohio. My curiosity, as with others, grew from Mark Twain's mythic narrative *The Adventures of Huckleberry Finn*—especially that crucial sixteenth chapter, in which Jim and Huck, the runaway black man and runaway white boy, adrift on the Mississippi, are looking for Cairo. Cairo, for Jim, represents a threshold to freedom; but the possibility of passing Cairo sets Huck to thinking of his moral responsibility.

> The river was very wide, and was walled with solid timber on both sides; you couldn't see a break in it hardly ever, or a light. We talked about Cairo, and wondered whether we would know it when we got to it. I said likely we wouldn't, because I had heard say there warn't but about a dozen houses there, and if they didn't happen to have them lit up, how was we going to know we was passing a town? Jim said if the two big rivers joined together there, that would show. But I said maybe we might think we was passing the foot of an island and coming into the same old river again. That disturbed Jim—and me too. So the question was, what to do?

Cairo posed a creative dilemma for the author. If the characters find the confluence and make their way up the Ohio, then
the narrative likely ends with no real development. If the current
takes them past it, they'll be carried deeper into slavery. Mark
Twain got to this point in his writing and did not know what to
do. The manuscript lay unfinished for years.

Cairo is called the "gateway to the South." What I found
was a city in ruins. I should have read more about its turbulent history. Cairo sits at the southernmost tip of Illinois,
funneled between these two great rivers. I came in from the
north, driving beneath an eighty-ton floodgate that can be
dropped to create an island completely surrounded by levees.
Remnants of Cairo's flourishing past were everywhere—the
sidewalks, churches, old mansions on "Millionaires Row," the
bank, the post office, the custom house museum. But there
was little commerce on Commercial Avenue. Many buildings
were crumbling or abandoned. It felt like the landscape of
some forgotten war.

I drove through town, across the southern levee, and past the
road that crosses to Kentucky. Just before I reached the bridge
that crosses to Missouri, I turned left on Fort Defiance Road
and into the park. Below, there was a flat spit of land coming to
a point.

This point provided a strategic defense during the American
Civil War. Within days of the shelling of Fort Sumter in April
1861, four regiments of Union soldiers were ordered to Cairo,
and construction of Camp Defiance got underway. By September, General Ulysses Grant had his headquarters here. Nothing
of the camp remains; but there was a lookout platform offering a
splendid, panoramic view. All around, the water was wide.

I was alone. From the tower platform, I could see where the waters meet. The Mississippi flowed in from the west. To the east, across the vast expanse of conjoined waters, I could see the green edges of Kentucky. Missouri extended south and spread to the west. Behind me, the long state of Illinois stretched north, all the way up to Lake Michigan. It was an awesome topography. I stood and watched as a tow with eighteen barges emerged from the Ohio, made a wide sweeping arc, and pointed itself toward the Mississippi.

Before the Civil War, Thomas Cram, a topographical engineer, wrote a book about Cairo, envisioning a great city at the heart of the nation. "There is no point in this Basin so strongly marked by nature as this for a great city," he wrote in 1851. "Cairo stands as a natural business mart between the geographical divisions of the north half and south half of the Mississippi Basin."

Steamboats converged here. The Illinois Central stopped here; more railroads were projected. Cram believed "Cairo would neither be a Northern nor a Southern city; it would be the central mart, where exchanges from the North, South, East and West, would take place; and by this commingling of commercial interests, a good influence would radiate thence in the four directions, to the remotest parts of the Republic."

After the war, the city prospered, and for decades seemed on track to realize Cram's vision. But as the town grew, so did the racial tensions and the violence. Organized crime found a home here. Eventually, the worst of the nation's exchanges overwhelmed the city's good influence, and by the 1960s, the disease and decay were very well advanced.

I crouched in the mud at the very point of confluence. I dipped my left hand in the Ohio River, and my right hand in the Mississippi. The waters seemed calm, stretching very far away and wide—to the south, to the west, to the east. I spread my fingers and felt for little eddies, any sign of the current's movement. All was still.

I stood and shook the water from my fingers and wiped them dry with a bandanna. There must be millions of stories embedded here. What creation stories emerged from the mud of this confluence? What tales did the indigenous Illinois tell of life's beginnings where the rivers met? If I listened long and patiently, could I hear the stories of those thousands of soldiers stationed here in the Civil War? Do the hopes and dreams yet linger, brought by so many African Americans—refugees from slavery, and then, decades later, those of the Great Migration, who rode the Illinois Central and got off at Cairo, the first stop in the north? What tales of sorrow and despair—of prostitutes, gamblers, drunkards, and addicts—have seeped into the mud of this enormous confluence?

There were murderers in Cairo, notorious lynchings. Some names are not forgotten. William "Froggie" James, a black man, was hanged one night in 1909, then shot when the rope broke, and beheaded, his body roasted and dismembered. On the very same night, Henry Salzner, a white man, was also hanged and shot in the public square. Such events brought civil rights advocate Ida B. Wells to Cairo. By the 1960s and '70s, corruption, crime, and violence were strangling Cairo. "It was dying slow and it was dying mean," said Ron Powers, the Pulitzer Prize–winning journalist who grew up in Hannibal and knows Cairo well. In 1991, he wrote, "The town's sulphurous legacy of corruption, wretched luck and murderous temperament made it seem cursed; a locus of evil."

There have been efforts to breathe new life into the city, and Powers described one such effort in his book *Far from Home*. But nothing has been truly effective. Then, in that exhausting and tumultuous year of 2020 that exposed so much of the nation's underbelly of racism, inequity, and intransigent polarization—a bright light shined on Cairo. Illinois governor J. B. Pritzker came to Cairo and announced that $40 million would be provided to build the Alexander-Cairo Port at the confluence. "This is more than just a port," the governor said. "It's also fuel for new jobs and new economic prosperity all across this region."

That visit from the governor would come more than a year after my solitary pilgrimage to Cairo. I stepped back from the point of confluence and walked slowly from the river's edge, up the gentle rise, toward a solitary tree. I stood and looked around. I thought of the sacred confluence of Bdote and remembered the stories I had heard there, and all that I had felt. I thought of other confluence sites—Prescott, Wyalusing, Grafton, Camp Dubois—and of so many more I hoped to see. I wished for a docent or storyteller to guide me.

And yet, on my own, I felt the pull of the four directions. And remembering Bdote, I wanted to respond with something like a prayer. But how, I wondered, and to whom?

I face the west, where the sun is sinking. I think of mountain streams, of creeks and rivers, rising from the plains and prairies, all pouring in and flowing past this point. I think of how the west, with its expansive, open spaces, shaped my young imagination. From the west, I developed a conviction that life held meaning and significance, of possibilities for tragedy and possibilities for blessing. I am grateful for the visionary spirit of the west.

I face the north, the land of lakes, my home for nearly forty years. I think of woods and solitude and wilderness—the north shore of Lake Superior, the greatest of all the lakes, and Lake Itasca, where the Mississippi starts. I think of life in the Twin Cities, of the urban affection I've acquired there, and a commitment to community. I think on the deaths of unarmed black men— Jamar Clark, Philando Castile, George Floyd—by armed police. I consider the anger that erupted from prolonged injustice and systemic racism. I am grateful for the scouring and solacing spirit of the north.

I face the east, where I was born, near the banks of the Ohio River, and where I drew my first breath and took my first steps. There, in the same Ohio River, Grandmother Ginevra took her final breath, drawing its waters into her lungs. From farther east, her ancestors came, in ships, then spread out, into the mountains of Appalachia and far beyond. Some became the owners of slaves, while others fought to end that curse. All of us joined the nation's mad appropriation of land. Where I now live, I watch the sun rise every morning above the Mississippi River. I give thanks for each new day. I am grateful for the dawning spirit of the east.

And then I face the south, where these waters go and warmth prevails. There is a warmth of climate, a warmth of temperament, and food so richly spiced, and scents of honeysuckle and magnolia. Those southern literary landscapes—of Faulkner, Conroy, Hurston, and O'Connor—and their stories, thickly layered, darkly nuanced. I am grateful for the fervent spirit of the south.

So there I stood, at the center of a vast and complex nation, between north and south, between east and west, and

I prayed for the restoration of this place. I prayed for the spirit of this nation. I prayed that from this confluence, goodness would radiate in four directions, even to the remotest parts of the Republic.

BEND

A Place of Awful Quiet

Like an old woman retelling the same story,
the Mississippi River remembers and remembers.

—"FLASHBACK" BY ANGELA SHANNON

1

U.S. HIGHWAY 61, THE CELEBRATED "BLUES HIGHWAY," first meets the Mississippi near my home and chases the river all the way down from Saint Paul to New Orleans, flirting first with one side and then the other. It caresses the curving underside of Lake Pepin. Then, as it descends through Wisconsin and Iowa, the highway keeps its distance, staying far back from the river's edge and out of sight. On the Iowa side of the river, a few miles north of Keokuk, just before the town of Montrose, the highway bends in toward the river for a brief, affectionate kiss. Here, the river swells to meet it, arching out from Illinois in a great sweeping bend around the Nauvoo point.

It's a roadside stop worth making—a spare and unassuming memorial to the beginning of the Mormon Trail. No covered wagons here, no statue, no museum—just a simple sign to mark the spot where, in the winter of 1846, thousands of Mormons crossed the frozen Mississippi, having abandoned their homes in Nauvoo to begin their long trek west to the Great Salt Lake. Through my binoculars, I gazed across the river at the restored temple, standing atop a green hill, gleaming, all white in the sunlight, and crowned by a touch of gold.

I had no plans to see Nauvoo. My interest was in the river and feeling its mythic presence. Besides, I thought I knew enough of Mormon history, and I was eager to get to Keokuk and on to Hannibal—following after Mark Twain back into Missouri. But standing at this crossroads of the Great River Road and the inauspicious beginning of the great Mormon Trail, my thoughts turned toward the west.

I pondered my own westward migration, driven, as a child, by my father's sudden, radical religious conversion. Reading the Gospels for the first time in his life, he took to heart the words of Jesus to a rich man: "Sell all you have, give to the poor . . . and follow me." So, my father did that, as he understood it. He sold what we had and took his young family east, from Ohio to New York, to study for the ministry. Then, he followed a faraway call to a very small church at a crossroads on the bleak high plains of eastern Wyoming. So, I grew up in the shadow of the church, on a vast, open landscape that gave shape to my spirit but slowly drained my mother's.

In time, my mother, like her mother before her, would die of despair. But, before that actually happened, we began edging our way eastward, retracing the Mormon Trail back along the North Platte River through the hills of western Nebraska. We spent some indolent years on the banks of the Frenchman Creek, skating its frozen stream in winter, watching the spring floods floating dead cows and debris past the tree house my brothers and I had built in a gigantic cottonwood.

And we moved again, farther east, all the way across Nebraska to the Missouri River and settled down in Omaha. From my mother's grave in Omaha's Forest Lawn cemetery, just off of Mormon Bridge Road, you can easily walk a few blocks to the Mormon Winter Quarters, where a temple now stands, and where that first wave of Mormon pioneers had stopped in 1846. Those pioneers had fled Nauvoo with Brigham Young after their prophet, Joseph Smith, was murdered. Hundreds of Mormons died of disease and winter's hardship and remain buried along the east bank of the Missouri River. That much I learned from my high school history class.

But now, while I sat at the roadside stop, brooding over the Mormon migration and the course of my own life, the sun sank behind me. Long shadows reached out across the river toward Nauvoo. So I pulled myself from my reverie and drove south a few more miles to Keokuk.

The next morning in Keokuk, I sought out any faint traces Mark Twain had left—the home where his mother, Jane Lampton Clemens, had lived until her death in 1890, and the place on Main Street where Orion Clemens had published the *Keokuk Journal*. There, a nineteen-year-old Sam Clemens had worked for his brother as a printer's apprentice before he took to the river. I lingered at the corner of First and Johnson, where a lodging house once stood, I was told, that overlooked the river and sheltered Sam Clemens in those apprentice days.

On the river, at Lock and Dam No. 19, I learned a bit about the Des Moines Rapids, which once stretched a dozen miles up from Keokuk to Nauvoo, stopping riverboat travelers at either end of the rapids. In Keokuk's Rand Park, I paused near the memorial to the Sauk chief Keokuk to hear someone talking to a group of young people about the Sauk and the Fox, about their migration here and displacement farther west. I heard of the conflict between Chief Keokuk and Black Hawk, of the rhetorical power of Keokuk's speeches, his skills of diplomacy, and his many efforts for peace. The speaker said that Keokuk once paddled across the river to visit Joseph Smith in Nauvoo and said to him, "I also am a son of the Great Spirit."

I spent the night in Keokuk. But when I got to Hannibal the next day, something seemed to be tugging me back to Nauvoo; so I did not stop there but crossed over the river into Illinois and headed back north on Highway 96, past Quincy, and on past dark, rolling fields just waiting for corn or soybeans to sprout.

At Warsaw, I followed the familiar signs for the Great River Road. Warsaw itself was a bleak, dispiriting town. The road through it drops sharply down to the river's edge. There is no riverfront, just a few shacks along the river's edge and two barges moored beside a silo. But the old Warsaw Road going north is a lovely stretch to drive. I imagined it looking very much the same in the nineteenth century, threading a way between sheer limestone walls on one side and the river's edge on the other.

In Nauvoo, I drove straight toward the gleaming temple, parked my car on Bluff Street, and walked around to the temple's entrance. The temple took dominion of everything around. It's an overwhelming structure, an imposing block of stone, scored with enormous pilasters and narrow windows, and topped by a chunky wedding cake of a spire. Three porticoes provide a bit of aesthetic relief.

I turned away and promptly forgot the temple, for the vista to the west simply took my breath. At the crest of the hill stands a large, contemplative sculpture of Joseph and Hyrum Smith on horseback, on the road toward Carthage to give themselves up to what they knew was certain death. Behind them, the green hill slopes down to the flats below, which are encircled by the silver arc of the river. Far beyond the encircling river, darker green bluffs rise and define the horizon.

Two days before, I found the view of Nauvoo from the river to be scenic; but the westward view from the hill is simply celestial. From the beginning, visitors have marveled at the beauty of this bend in the river. When Samuel Prior, a Methodist minister, came to Nauvoo in 1843, he said that the hill and the plain "pushing itself into the river" reminded him of a fairy land.

Each summer, historic Nauvoo fills with Mormon pilgrims for whom this landscape is sacred. On one such trip, the late LDS president Gordon B. Hinckley gave voice to the prophetic significance he saw in "the great sweeping bend of the Mississippi with the city standing as it were on a peninsula eagerly reaching out, pointing to the West, where the people who lived there would go."

There is a rhetorical power in this topography, explains Seth Perry, an American religious historian, which was crucial to the formation of Mormon identity in the early 1840s—especially as rumors of polygamy began to roil the region. He writes:

> To Mormons, the stirring view of the river from the high bluffs of Nauvoo and the view of the city's temple from the river endorsed a providential view of themselves and of their leader. At the same time, the fact that outsiders could view the same scene with a sharp sense of dissonance—lamenting that a scurrilous religion had profaned a beautiful river setting—points to the importance of deliberate rhetorical efforts in making the river bend into a Mormon symbol.

What the great river bend would symbolize to Mormons varied greatly over time; but its deepest significance cannot be defined by Mormon ideology alone. A bend or oxbow will shape any stream's mystique—whether it's a swiftly flowing river or a meandering creek. Roads and train tracks have this effect, too—something "comin' round the bend" stirs an expectation of change. As an outsider, my experience of this landscape will not reflect a Mormon point of view.

The temple behind me was shut, and the mysteries of its interior forbidden. But the topography awakened something within me. I walked away from the temple, down Mulholland Street, descending the hill into the streets of old Nauvoo.

2

When Joseph Smith settled this site in 1839, having been driven from Missouri, and earlier from Ohio and elsewhere, a small collection of buildings was already established, known as Commerce. The flats surrounding the hill were mosquito-laden swamps. Smith renamed the place Nauvoo (claiming the word meant "beautiful place"), and within five years, he and his disciples had drained the swamps and built a city to rival Chicago.

What stretched before me seemed, at first, like a quaint college campus—a collection of small, brick buildings scattered over a vast expanse of trees and grass. I entered a grove where, according to a posted sign, Joseph Smith would preach to his followers. I stopped and sat among the trees just beginning to leaf. Here, the prophet preached his most famous sermon, the so-called King Follett Discourse, occasioned by the death of an elder who had been crushed in a well. Smith's sermon began with these words:

> Because the wind blows very hard, it will hardly be possible for me to make you all hear unless I have your profound attention.

I approach a matter of the greatest importance and the most solemn of any that can occupy our attention—that is, the subject of the dead.

A crowd of some twenty thousand sat in the grove that evening to hear the prophet speak. Joseph Smith's six-foot height and penetrating blue eyes gave him a commanding presence. There was a magnetism in his speech, a mixture of coarseness and elegance most listeners found compelling. On this night, his sermon was bold and startling, declaring God, who sits in heaven, "is a man like one of you." But it was also, as he said, a sermon about the dead. "The greatest responsibility in this world that God has laid upon us is to seek after our dead," he said. In less than ninety days, Smith would himself be dead, murdered by an angry mob.

Now, all was silent in the grove except for the sighing of the wind. It was April, and there were no visitors in sight. I left the grove and walked on down the hill through what once had been a vibrant city. Blocks of land lay vacant, except for the trees— hickory and oak, walnut and ash, planted in regular formation, suggesting the faint grid work of houses and streets. I felt a mysterious presence.

In the autumn of 1846, two years after Joseph Smith's murder, a twenty-two-year-old attorney named Thomas Kane traveled up the Mississippi River and stood, enchanted by the glittering city he glimpsed from the other side of the river's bend. His steamboat had been halted at Keokuk by low water and the turbulent Des Moines Rapids, and so he arrived in Montrose by carriage. Looking across the river, Kane took in the beauty of the buildings, the green gardens, and the "noble marble edifice, whose high tapering spire was radiant with white and gold." He determined to row across the river to see it. What Kane described was like a scene straight from *The Twilight Zone*:

> I procured a skiff, and rowing across the river, landed at the chief wharf of the city. No one met me there. I looked, and saw no one. I could hear no one move; though the quiet everywhere was such that I heard the flies buzz, and the water-ripples break against the shallow of the beach. I walked through the solitary streets. The town lay as in a dream, under some deadening spell of loneliness, from which I almost feared to wake it. For plainly it had not slept long. There was no grass growing up in the paved ways. Rains had not entirely washed away the prints of dusty footsteps.
>
> Yet I went about unchecked. I went into empty workshops, rope walks and smithies. The spinner's wheel was idle; the carpenter had gone from his workbench and shavings, his unfinished sash and casing. Fresh bark was in the tanner's vat, and the fresh-chopped lightwood stood piled against the baker's oven. The blacksmith's shop was cold; but his coal heap and ladling pool and crooked water horn were all there, as if he had just gone off for a holiday. No work people anywhere looked to know my errand. If I went into the gardens . . . no one called out to me from any opened window, or dog sprang forward to bark an alarm. I could have supposed the people hidden in the houses, but the doors were unfastened; and when at last I timidly entered them, I found dead ashes white upon the hearths, and had to tread a tiptoe, as if walking down the aisle of a country church, to avoid rousing irreverent echoes from the naked floors.

The Nauvoo I found is a haunting place, too—though nothing like the abandoned city Thomas Kane encountered. Coal heap and ladling pool, gardens and unfastened doors have all disappeared. Foundations have been filled, the decay has been purged and the rubble removed. Blacksmith's shop and baker's oven have been restored and are open to tourists, as are some of the homesteads. And the great temple itself, destroyed by arson in 1848 and toppled by a tornado two years later, was eventually rebuilt and rededicated in 2002.

What I experienced was an awful, palpable stillness, as powerful as the chambers and kivas of Chaco Canyon, or the grassy corridors of Glastonbury Abbey. It doesn't take much to stir the imagination. The scattered relics I encountered as a child on the high plains of Wyoming could open doorways into the past—stone tipi rings, flint fragments lying undisturbed beneath sagebrush, abandoned windmills, empty mine shafts, a solitary abandoned church, the scars of old highways and trails.

When a twenty-three-year-old artist from England, Frederick Piercy, steamed up the Mississippi to Nauvoo in 1853, he recorded what he saw, stepping off the boat: "On the banks of the river lie broken blocks of stone and shattered bricks, and the visitors' first steps are over evidences of ruin and desolation. Foundations of what must once have been substantial buildings are broken up and exposed to the light." Piercy's detailed sketches and engravings endure as a beautiful memorial to the Mormon migration. In Nauvoo, now, no shattered bricks or decaying ruins remain, no dust lies thick and undisturbed. The physical record of that city's life has largely been rubbed out, leaving only the faint gridlines of streets to serve as an idealized map for a score of reconstructed buildings.

The sweeping bend of the river and the surrounding cottonwoods suggest an air of serenity and calm in old Nauvoo. And yet, it's still a very unsettling place. This is not the sentimental "bend in the river where the cottonwoods grow" John Wayne spoke of in *War of the Wildcats*. This is a land soaked in sadness and death. As I sat in the sacred grove, I thought I could hear the persistent sounds of weeping; but it must have been only my imagination. I saw no moving forms around me.

The next morning, I came back to Nauvoo and fell into conversation with one of the LDS sisters in the restored home of Brigham Young.

"Thomas," she asked after chatting with me for some time from the other side of Brigham's dining room table, "have you felt a presence here?"

"I have indeed," I replied. She waited for more, but I remained silent.

"Well," she said quietly, "that's the Holy Spirit you are sensing." She reached across the table and gave me a copy of the Book of Mormon. "Take it," she said, "and read it."

There is an awful stillness in Nauvoo. Whether the spirit of this place is a "holy" one or some other kind of spirit, its presence gripped me fiercely. I began to think there might be something it could teach me. At the very least, I hoped to learn how the river shaped—and has been shaped by—the life and the death of Nauvoo.

Something caught hold of Thomas Kane and held him firmly. He would follow the Mormons to Utah and establish a deep friendship with Brigham Young. He would devote much of his life to advocating their causes. He would become an ardent abolitionist and later would be gravely wounded in the American Civil War. But Thomas Kane never did become a Mormon.

3

As with any thrilling ghost story, murder lies at the heart of Nauvoo's history. I set out to contemplate the murder—or the martyrdom, some would say—of Joseph and Hyrum Smith. I wanted to see where they had died.

The half-hour drive from Nauvoo to Carthage crosses a plain of unbearable flatness. The old Carthage road that Joseph and Hyrum took to surrender themselves to the sheriff is mostly buried beneath cultivated fields. But there are some pilgrims, I've been told, who trace that old road across those fields. I arrived at the Carthage jailhouse, paid my admission, and joined a group just beginning the tour. There was an elder in a gray suit with sharply pressed trousers, who welcomed us and said he'd like to begin by reading a passage from Mosiah, in the Book of Mormon. It's a passage about a prophet named Abinadi, he explained, who was martyred "because he would not deny the commandments of God, having sealed the truth of his words by his death."

The elder closed the book and gazed upon our reverent group, very like the way my father would look out from his pulpit across his congregation. "The mob thought to seal the fate of the saints," the elder said, "but like Jesus and the prophets of old, he sealed the truth of his words by his death. Where you are is sacred ground." Then the elder invited us in to see the place.

I found myself beside a window in the second-floor bedroom above the jail cells. Here, the elder explained, the jailer had taken the four saints who had surrendered themselves—the two who would be killed, and the two who would be witnesses. The jailer feared leaving them exposed in the cells below and thought the four would be safer in his bedroom upstairs. But the mob got to them anyway. The elder showed us the hole in the door made by the bullet that killed Hyrum.

"And there," the elder said, pointing to where I stood, "the prophet fell through the window into the yard below, shot both in the back, by the men storming up the stairs, and in the front, by the mob outside." Someone asked about bloodstains that long had darkened the floor but were no longer visible. "They removed the stain," the elder said, "because it was considered much too graphic."

Journalist Alex Beam calls the murder of Joseph Smith an *American crucifixion*. "The assassination of Joseph Smith marked the beginning of the triumphal Mormon progress that continues to this day," he writes. "Joseph's death did not paralyze the Mormons. Instead, it galvanized the Saints."

I'd hear that perspective again and again in Nauvoo—the story of triumphal Mormon progress. Since then, I have come to hear other, often conflicting, stories. I discovered the presence of death permeates the Mormon story more deeply than I could imagine, even if the graphic bloodstains and the rubble had not been removed. In the early years of Nauvoo, for example, mortality from malaria alone was frightfully high, especially in 1841. And after Nauvoo, the experience of death persisted westward. Some six hundred graves were dug in the Winter Quarters of 1846/47, on the western banks of the Missouri river, and countless unmarked graves were strung along the trail. Death not only drove Smith's theology, it galvanized the westward march of the Mormons.

Samuel Morris Brown is a University of Utah physician who teaches pulmonary and critical care medicine. Dr. Brown has written a book on the early Mormon conquest of death, placing Smith's construction of immortal communities within a larger antebellum context of death and the dead. The Mormon scriptures Smith transcribed are themselves "largely derived from grave artifacts," Brown observes, "entombed gold plates" which "gave voice to America's dead in the 1830 Book of Mormon."

Coming to terms with death lies at the core of all religious systems, says Mary Ann Meyers, a religious historian and senior fellow at the John Templeton Foundation. But "the faith which sustained the Mormons in the darkest hours of their pilgrimage was an unquestioning faith in the reality of eternal progression. The Mormons' beliefs about death cannot be understood apart from their conviction, expressed over and over again, that improvement was inevitable if man kept working towards it."

Literary folks have not thought highly of the Book of Mormon. Mark Twain considered it a "curiosity" and called it "an insipid mess of inspiration." My copy is now shelved among the American romantics, beside the darker tales of Poe and Hawthorne who composed their best short works in the years of Mormonism's explosive growth. "Joseph Smith's is a complicated story with many twists and turns and possible interpretive approaches," says Dr. Brown. "However tempting it is to call him a Romantic expressing an excessive nostalgia for past epochs, though, Smith was not merely venerating the past. The Mormon prophet was actively seeking out the dead, both past and future, and placing them into direct family relationships with himself." Joseph Smith, he adds, was a man "roaring in the face of death."

I left Carthage and drove back to Nauvoo. I learned that the bullet-riddled bodies of Joseph and Hyrum Smith had been carried from Carthage to Nauvoo in straw-filled wagons. Thousands had lined the streets to mourn. The bullet wounds were plugged, their bodies washed, then dressed and laid out in the dining room of the Mansion House. Witnesses said that, in the heat of that late June day, blood continued to seep out of the wounds, pooled on the floor, and stuck to the shoes of those filing by the caskets.

Emma Smith, then about five months pregnant with David, locked the doors to the mansion after the viewing ended that Saturday night. Several trusted friends removed the bodies from the coffins and replaced them with sand, for they had ample reason to fear the bodies might be stolen or desecrated—and not only by outsiders. "Emma feared that Brigham [Young] might try to seize Joseph's corpse to legitimize his claim to be continuing Joseph's legacy," says Dr. Brown. "She was right." The coroner delivered the sand-filled coffins to the Nauvoo cemetery, and guards were stationed to complete the deception. After midnight, however, the bodies were carried across the street and secretly buried in the basement of the unfinished Nauvoo House hotel. Construction debris and litter was scattered over the graves to hide them. And that night, heavy rains obliterated all evidence of the basement burial. In the days that followed, says Dr. Brown, the Mormons came to accept Smith's death because they imagined him with them, looking after them from beyond.

Some months after the murder, around Christmastime, Emma Smith secretly exhumed the corpses and reburied them west of the Smith homestead, close to the river, beneath a small shed. Emma's bones would join theirs when she died in 1879. And many years later, when the Mississippi River began to rise behind the newly constructed Lock and Dam No. 19, their graves had been all but forgotten. It took engineers a week in 1928 to find them and move the bodies up to higher ground, close to the homestead!

I wandered freely through the open spaces of Nauvoo, trying to absorb all that I had learned, and listened to the land, hoping it would speak. The story of the fall of Nauvoo felt like a Gothic tale, but the landscape itself felt biblical. The word *desolation* asserted itself, and in turn, pried from the recesses of my memory, vague scriptural passages I must have read, long ago, in my more devotional years—from the prophets, "Your holy cities have become a wilderness, Zion has become a wilderness, Jerusalem a desolation." And from the Psalms, "Come, behold the works of the Lord; see what desolations he has brought on the earth."

4

On Water Street, very close to the river, I came across an excavated cellar enclosed by a picket fence, marking the spot where the town's newspaper, the *Times and Seasons*, was published in the early years of Nauvoo. The foundation is about five feet deep, built of layered limestones and overgrown with weeds. When archaeologists from the University of Missouri excavated the site in the 1970s, they found the basement filled with detritus from the early twentieth century: bottles, cans, buckets, tiles, license plates, and other rubbish; but they also uncovered projectile points and human bone from some unknown, prehistoric burial site, plundered to use as fill.

I leaned on the picket fence and studied my long shadow stretching across the foundation. I pondered all I had heard and experienced that day, and thought about the times and the seasons in which I now live. The air was becoming chilly.

Earlier, I had paused a few blocks north and east at the corner of Kimball and Main, to see the restored buildings of the printing house and the home of John Taylor, the editor of *Times and Seasons* and one of the wounded witnesses to Joseph Smith's murder. There, a pair of Latter-day Saints regaled me with stories about the life and influence of John Taylor—his move from England to Toronto to Missouri to Nauvoo, and his going back to England and Ireland as a Mormon missionary. They spoke of Taylor's spiritual journey from Anglicanism to Methodism and finally to Mormonism. "Truth will prevail," they said; it was the motto of the *Times and Seasons*. I also learned of the *Nauvoo Neighbor* and the *Wasp*, other publications Taylor edited. They showed me some excerpts of his writing, and I was impressed. Taylor would become the Mormon's third president, the Thomas Jefferson of the Mormon Church. Still, something seemed missing from the narrative. Nothing could account for the sense of desolation I was feeling all around me. Later, I would learn what was not told to me—the story of William Law and the *Nauvoo Expositor*, and the real reason the saints were driven from Nauvoo.

Before I left Nauvoo, I walked a short distance farther west on Water Street, along the edge of the Mississippi River, until I came to the site of the former ferry crossing where Water Street joins up with Parley. There stands a monument and a split-rail fence edging Parley Street, designating the road as the "Exodus to Greatness." A replica of the ferry stands nearby.

Here the river flows silently. "What can you tell me about the river?" I would ask the elders and the sisters I encountered.

And again, I would hear the tale of triumphal progress, of the river's providential freezing near the end of February of '46, so the wagons could cross over. I heard of the gathering of wagons at Sugar Creek camp, just a few miles into the Iowa territory. And the hero of that story was always Brigham Young.

> Lo! a mighty host of Jacob
> Tented on the western shore
> Of the noble Mississippi,
> Which they had been crossing o'er;
> At the last day's dawn of winter,
> Bound with frost and wrapt in snow:
> Hark! the sound is onward, onward!
> Camp of Israel! rise and go.

Eliza R. Snow penned those words the first Sunday in March of 1846, the day the Saints left Sugar Creek camp for the long trek west across the Iowa territory. At that time, by crossing the Mississippi, the Mormons actually were leaving the United States. So, the river became a mythic marker—their Jordan, their Rubicon, their Delaware and Ohio. In time, I would learn much more about Eliza Snow, the plural wife to both Joseph Smith and Brigham Young, the woman who became the Mormon bard, composing songs of Zion all the way to the promised land.

5

A year and a half later, I returned to Nauvoo—intentionally, this time. I had some unfinished business with this bend in the river. Throughout the long winter nights in Minnesota, I had been reading books on Nauvoo—Jon Krakauer's sensational chapter in *Under the Banner of Heaven*, Alex Beam's *American Crucifixion*, and Benjamin Pykles's book on historical archaeology, *Excavating Nauvoo*. And then I discovered Emma—Emma Hale Smith—through a brilliant biography called *Mormon Enigma* by Linda King Newell and Valeen Tippetts Avery.

These books gave words to the sorrow I'd merely felt and filled gaps in the narrative I'd only partly heard. In Nauvoo, the tellers of the tale said much to me about those formative years before 1839—visions of the prophet, the gold plates and translation, missionary endeavors and accompanying persecution—and even more was said, with greater joy, about the Saints' departure in 1846 and their triumphal journey west. But the middle span of seven years was presented to me as transition, not as a crucial tragedy. Were this history a novel, the seven Nauvoo years would comprise the middle passage. Were it a Shakespearean tragedy, this would be the complex, dramatic third act.

On those cold winter nights in Minnesota, I read of a man who would be king, who had called himself "King of the Kingdom of God and His Laws with the Keys and powers thereof," who built hotels and who passionately—though ineptly—pursued commerce and real estate, who frequently took advantage of vulnerable women and lied about his relations with them, who loved military parades, who polarized his followers and, in the end, violently suppressed the exercise of a free press, defying the laws and the democratic values of these United States. And he announced himself as a candidate for president of the United States!

Most of Smith's doctrines and revelations that would shape Mormon theology emerged from these tumultuous Nauvoo years, including baptism for the dead and the doctrine and practice of plural marriage. It was, of course, a time of tremendous duplicity and contradiction.

"This burst of theological inspiration coincided with an extended eruption of libidinous energy," writes Jon Krakauer. "Between 1840 and 1844 God instructed the prophet to marry some forty women. Most were shocked and revolted when Joseph revealed what the Lord had in mind for them. Several were still pubescent girls."

Rumors of Smith's dalliances had dogged him from the outset. In 1832 in Ohio, a mob actually dragged the prophet from his bed, stripped him, and threatened castration; but they let him go with a tarring and feathering. Privately, in Nauvoo, Smith used a revelation from God to justify his seductions; but publicly, he denied any practice of polygamy. Emma, however, was devastated, though publicly, she, too, would always deny that Joseph had taken any woman but herself. Emma must have felt increasingly isolated by the scandals. "Joseph's choice of women as plural wives gradually put a wedge between Emma and her friends," explain Linda Newell and Valeen Avery. "By late summer 1843 most of Emma's friends had either married Joseph or had given their daughters to him."

It all came to a crisis when Joseph propositioned Jane, the beloved wife of William Law, Smith's counselor. Law had contributed much to Nauvoo's success. But when he objected to Smith's immoral behavior, the prophet had him excommunicated. William Law then purchased and set up his own printing press on the corner of Mulholland and Page, very close to the temple site. William Law was joined by his brother, Wilson, and by Dr. Robert Foster, a prominent physician who had built the beautiful Mansion House for the Smiths; but then Dr. Foster, too, caught Smith attempting to seduce his wife. On June 7, 1844, the Laws and the Fosters published the first and the only issue of the *Nauvoo Expositor*, exposing what they considered Smith's sexual, financial, and political wrongdoings. Many in the town were angered—not at Smith but at the *Expositor*. Smith ordered the city marshal to destroy Law's press, and at night, a mob of men trashed the offices of the *Expositor*, smashed the printing press with sledgehammers, and burned its papers and furnishings in the street.

People outside Nauvoo were outraged. Stories had been seeping out of Nauvoo for some time. On June 21, the governor of Illinois, Thomas Ford, came to Carthage, and the next day wrote to Smith and the city council of Nauvoo:

> I now express to you my opinion that your conduct in the destruction of the press was a very gross outrage upon the laws and the liberties of the people. It may have been full of libels, but this did not authorize you to destroy it.
>
> There are many newspapers in this state which have been wrongfully abusing me for more than a year, and yet such is my regard for the liberty of the press and the rights of a free people in a republican government that I would shed the last drop of my blood to protect those presses from any illegal violence.

Within a week, Joseph Smith was dead. I began to grasp the awful quiet of Nauvoo. And I began to reflect on the times and the seasons in which I am living. I thought of the fading of civil discourse, the charges of "fake news," the assaults on journalists and freedom of the press, the mania for owning guns and the violence they make possible, the hypocrisy of political leaders who disregard democratic values, the complicity of the righteous who murder truth in the name of righteousness and stir up fear to feed their hunger for power.

So, I had come back to Nauvoo, this great bend in the river, to listen to what it might say to me. It was autumn. I did not drive to the temple hill as before, but rather, I went down to the old ferry crossing where Water Street meets Parley. I parked my car and stood next to the river, listening to the wind sighing through the willows and rustling the cottonwoods. Impulsively, I took off my shoes and stepped into the Mississippi River itself. The water was warmer than I had expected. I rolled my jeans up past my kneecaps and moved a bit farther into the stream.

6

Charlotte Haven came to Nauvoo in January of 1843, not as a Mormon but to join her brother, who had secured a house and a business here. Charlotte was twenty-three. Traveling by stage up from Quincy, she nearly lost her life at Warsaw when the horses slipped and plunged down the steep, icy road, careening over the riverbank and onto the frozen Mississippi.

Charlotte called Nauvoo "a city of fanatics," and found it to be "a collection of miserable houses and hovels." But she stayed on for a year, writing descriptive letters to her parents in New Hampshire, including this account of a walk along the Mississippi River one Sunday morning in the spring of 1843:

> We followed the bank toward town, and rounding a little point covered with willows and cottonwoods, we spied quite a crowd of people, and soon perceived there was a baptism. Two

elders stood knee-deep in the icy water, and immersed one after another as fast as they could come down the bank. We soon observed that some of them went in and were plunged several times. We were told that they were baptized for the dead who had not had the opportunity of adopting the doctrines of the Latter Day Saints. So these poor mortals in ice-cold water were releasing their ancestors and relatives from purgatory! We drew a little nearer and heard several names repeated by the elders as the victims were douched, and you can imagine our surprise when the name George Washington was called. So after these fifty years he is out of purgatory and on his way to the "celestial" heaven! It was enough, and we continued our walk homeward.

Half a century later, an aged Wilford Woodruff—who had once owned a hat shop in Nauvoo and later became the fourth LDS president—stood in the Salt Lake City tabernacle and reminisced:

Joseph Smith himself . . . went into the Mississippi river one Sunday night after meeting, and baptized a hundred. I baptized another hundred. The next man, a few rods from me, baptized another hundred. We were strung up and down the Mississippi, baptizing for our dead.

So, here I was, back in Nauvoo a year and a half after my first visit, standing in the silent pull of the Mississippi River on a brilliant autumn morning, thinking about those baptism scenes—comedy for Haven, sacred nostalgia for Woodruff. I imagined all those people, themselves now long dead, strung along the edge of this great bend in the river, calling out to connect with the souls of America's dead. The awful quiet of Nauvoo deepened.

7

I walked along Water Street to the Smith homestead and stood before the graves of Joseph, Hyrum, and Emma Smith. One large, inclined granite monument serves for all three, with identical inscriptions carved into both sides of the stone—the vertical face, and the opposite, sloping face of the stone. I had passed by here on my earlier visit, but had not lingered then. Now, I studied the inscriptions. Emma's grave was nearest the river.

EMMA HALE SMITH

WIFE OF JOSEPH SMITH, JR.

BORN HARMONY, PENNSYLVANIA

JULY 10, 1804

DIED NAUVOO, ILLINOIS

APRIL 30, 1879

Joseph and Hyrum, of course, had died on the same day in 1844, but Emma lived thirty-five more years, dying a couple of months shy of her seventy-fifth birthday. Her life in Nauvoo had spanned forty years.

Forty years! I stood and pondered this length of time. In biblical tradition, forty years is symbolic. A span of forty—whether forty days and forty nights, or forty years—was not necessarily intended to be a precise designation. It could stand for a long, indefinite passage of time, but the specificity of *forty* always indicated the time as being spiritually significant. I began to think about what this forty-year span must have meant for Emma. How could she, the "elect lady" of the Mormons—for whom community would be everything—endure a life in a place of such awful blankness? How did she carry on amid the inexorable decay of homes and livelihoods she had known and helped to build? What kept her rooted when everything around her was being uprooted? What nourished her faith when the church she helped nourish simply moved on, and the congregation, for whom she had compiled a hymnal, was no longer present to sing out its hymns?

I don't know how long I stood before Emma's grave, pondering these questions, before I felt the presence of someone standing near, on the sloping side of the monument. I looked up and blurted out something like, "How could she do it? How did she ever keep going?"

The man on the other side of the grave did not immediately respond, and I had not really expected to get a reply. It was simply one of those moments when, as in a crowd or atop some scenic overlook, we see a wonderful sight and feel compelled to express our wonder to any person nearby. The man looked down at the grave for what seemed a long time. When he looked up, it was not at me but toward the south where the great river sparkled.

"Emma had the river." His face was kind and thoughtful, a visage so relaxed it seemed ageless. "She loved the Mississippi River."

What my own countenance may have conveyed, I cannot know; but my heart cried out silently, *Please tell me more!* He introduced himself as William; he wore no badge, but the words *Community of Christ* were stitched above the pocket of his blue denim shirt. He seemed so free and so easy, I wondered if he really was a docent or just another visitor. But he offered to guide me through the properties.

We entered the log homestead Joseph and Emma lived in when they came to Nauvoo in the spring of 1839. William told me of Emma's having walked from Missouri to Quincy, Illinois, crossing the frozen Mississippi River in February 1839—without Joseph, bringing horses and a wagon, and her four young children. There, in Quincy, Emma waited until her husband could escape from his imprisonment in Missouri. He told me about their early life in the homestead, struggles with malaria, the death of two more of their children (Emma had already buried three), and the explosive growth of the community of Saints.

Within four years, the Smiths were moving across the street to the beautiful Mansion House that Dr. Foster built, a white, two-story building in the Greek Revival style. Quite frankly, I don't remember all that William told me, so vigorously had my imagination been stirred by my earlier, winter reading. It must have been a turbulent year in the Mansion House—less than a year—before Joseph's body would be laid out in the dining room, dripping blood onto the floor.

I imagined that year of countless visitors from the town, tourists from the riverboats, the carriages coming and going, the banquets and the weddings. Charlotte Haven, the young woman who earlier was amused by the river baptisms, described an October afternoon banquet at the Mansion House she attended with her Mormon neighbor, a Mr. Hollister:

> He called me in his buggy at eleven o'clock in the forenoon and drove direct to the Mansion. Joseph came forward to assist me from the carriage. I was ushered upstairs to the dressing-room, and then sent down to the parlor where were seated about thirty elderly ladies and a number of young married ones holding

babies, with none of whom was I acquainted. A more vacant, unintellectual company I had never met . . . A great many of them wore around their necks a string of gold or gilded beads the size of peas, the only jewelry except marriage rings seen here. As usual not much was said, and as for exchange of ideas I don't think there was any. One pale-faced creature says to another in a peculiar drawl, "How do you do; sister M.?"

"Why, I am just getting over a long fit of sickness. How is your health, sister R.?"

"Why, this is the first time I've been out since having the fever."

"How miserable you look, sister B."

"Yes, I ain't well. I have a heap of misery in my side and am powerful weak all over."

"What a curious-shaped head your child's got!" And much more of the same sort.

When dinner was announced at one o'clock, Charlotte writes, there were 120 couples. "Two long tables extending the length of the room were loaded with good substantial food. The women were on one side and their partners opposite. Joseph and Emma took part with several young girls in waiting on the guests."

Always, in Joseph's life, there seemed to be young girls about, and older women, too. I asked William about the tumult surrounding Joseph's other women, but on this topic, he was reticent. There are several accounts of Emma shoving Eliza Snow, "heavy with child," down the central staircase of the Mansion House. They had been friends until Emma discovered Eliza had secretly married Joseph. Newell and Avery report that Emma, for a time, apparently came to terms with Joseph's insistence on plural marriage. "In May 1843 she finally agreed to give Joseph other wives if she could choose them . . . Emma chose the two sets of sisters then living in her house, Emily and Eliza Partridge and Sarah and Maria Lawrence." But there would be others she did not choose.

William led me from the Mansion House and away from whatever ghosts might yet be haunting it. We paused beside the white picket fence at the corner of Water and Main, where all was still. I was lost in my own emotions, imagining Emma's psychic pain and the anguish of other women as the doctrine of plural marriage began to surface in Nauvoo. It was clear that Emma had found polygamy repulsive, but her devotion to Joseph seemed equally strong. She and her children had continued living in the Mansion House after Joseph's death and through the months of the Mormon exodus as the city emptied out.

8

"And now the house I find the most fascinating," William said. We strolled across Water Street and walked beside a low stone cottage bearing a sign "Bidamon Stable" (a private residence), and came to the large, redbrick house built upon a white stone foundation. "Unfortunately, we can't go in, as it's being used by a group of students; but I can tell you something about it."

"Isn't this where Emma buried Joseph and Hyrum in the unfinished basement?" I asked.

William nodded. "As with the temple, Joseph Smith never saw its completion. But he seemed to think its presence as important as the temple; he said God told him to build it." William paused and spread his hands wide like a dramatic prophet of old: *"And let the name of that house be called Nauvoo House, and let it be a delightful habitation for man, and a resting place for the weary traveler, that he may contemplate the glory of Zion."*

William smiled and dropped his hands. "Well, weary travelers came here anyway, before he'd built this house, and he put them up, back there in the Mansion House. It would be for Emma and her second husband, Lewis Bidamon, to finish Nauvoo House. They called it Riverside Mansion, which I think is a more fitting name." William paused thoughtfully. "It was the river that built Nauvoo as much as the prophet's vision."

I asked William what he meant, and he began a meandering explanation of how historic Nauvoo must be seen as a river town as much as a religious community. He reminded me that Nauvoo's growth coincided with the expansion of steamboating, from the 1830s through the 1850s. "Most of those houses that once stood there," he said, pointing toward the great open areas to the north, "were built of wood—log cabins, pine shacks, even the brick homes needed framing. All that lumber was brought down the river from Wisconsin. Food, tourists, all the commodities needed to keep this town going, either came up the river or down the river. Sometimes three or four steamboats a day would stop at Nauvoo. And in 1843, Nauvoo got its own steamboat, the *Maid of Iowa.*"

William told of a Captain Dan Jones, who had just purchased a small stern-wheeler, about one hundred feet long. In New Orleans, he agreed to bring a couple of hundred British immigrants—recent Mormon converts—up the river to Nauvoo. Soon after they arrived at the Nauvoo House dock, the captain and the prophet became friends. So, Captain Jones became a Mormon, and Smith acquired a steamboat! In the months that followed, the *Maid of Iowa* was "a real workhorse for Nauvoo, bringing several thousand more immigrants upstream, providing ferry service across the river, and occasionally offering pleasure excursions on the river."

"Would Nauvoo have kept growing . . . ?" I ventured.

"Had the Saints not left?" he completed my question, then shrugged. "It wasn't really an option. Even so, growth was not sustainable as it was. There had been ongoing talk about building a dam to harness the river's power. Some considered digging a canal straight through the town along Main Street; but, in the end, nothing came of it. Nauvoo would have needed to develop some kind of industry or commerce." William fell silent.

"But the Nauvoo House was finished," I prompted, hoping he would tell me more about Emma and her love of the river. The pages of my notebook rustled in the breeze.

William suggested we sit on the grass near the edge of the cul-de-sac at the end of Main Street. It was a grassy slope on what seemed to be a small levee running along the edge of the river. From where we sat, looking north, we could see Emma's three homes, each on a corner of Water Street and Main: the log homestead to our left, about one hundred feet back, and the red Nauvoo House to our right. North of Nauvoo House, past the Bidamon Stable and across Water Street, stood the white Mansion House. This trio of homes had defined Emma's world for forty years.

William loafed on the sloping grass, silent for several minutes. The sun, behind us, warmed the earth where we sat. Then he resumed his story, which I'll try to recast in my own words as best as I can recall.

9

By the end of the summer of '46, life in Nauvoo felt truly apocalyptic. Much of the city had been abandoned; some of the deserted houses had been plundered. Various groups of people freely came and went. The town grew rough and dangerous. And while the American Civil War was still fifteen years in the future, another kind of civil war was erupting in Nauvoo—between Mormons who remained and a growing force of anti-Mormons who sought to drive out any trace of Mormonism.

Emma, too, made preparation to leave—not for the west, as nothing could induce her to join Brigham Young, she said—but upstream to Fulton, where she had some friends. Emma rented out the Mansion House, disposed of some of her property, and waited. Steamboats had been warned not to dock at Nauvoo. But one Saturday in September, a courageous captain docked his side-wheeler packet boat to take on passengers. Emma boarded this boat, the *Uncle Toby*, with her children, determined never to return. She would leave Nauvoo as she had come, without her husband and with children in tow.

It wasn't long before anti-Mormon forces invaded, desecrating the temple and forcing the remaining Mormons to surrender. In spite of the state's efforts to keep peace, there was resistance and there was blood.

Emma had just settled in to her new life in Fulton when she received a letter from a man with whom she and Joseph had previously done business. Lewis Bidamon was seeking to rent out the Mansion House, which Emma already had leased.

Emma wrote him back immediately, saying the mansion had been leased, but she had other properties to rent.

Time passed, and Emma received no payment from the man who'd leased the Mansion House. So, she arranged for a carriage and took her children back to Nauvoo, arriving at the Mansion House just in time to catch the tenant in the act of removing her furnishings.

Lewis, too, came back to Nauvoo, and soon he and Emma began to see each other. Lewis was not the kind of man you'd expect would interest Emma very much. He was tall, like Joseph, and some say rather handsome. But he was not a Mormon—not even religious, though he had respected Mormons and had been a member of the militia sent by the state to try to keep peace in Nauvoo. He was neither well educated nor very successful. Twice he had been married; and he had something of a reputation for liquor and gambling. But two days before Christmas of 1847, Emma and Lewis married and remained together for the rest of Emma's life.

There were challenges, as you'd expect in setting up a home life together: Lewis brought his young daughters to join Emma's children. Emma took in Joseph's aged mother, Lucy Mack Smith. The children from both sides grew up, sometimes married well, sometimes not; some left, then moved back home. David, Emma's youngest, was a sensitive and creative soul who slowly went mad and eventually would die in an asylum. When Emma and Lewis had been married for some years—Emma was into her sixties—Lewis fathered a child by a woman from a nearby town. But Emma, in a remarkable act of compassion and forgiveness, took in this young child, and a few years later, the child's mother, named Nancy. It is reported that, on her deathbed, Emma actually encouraged Lewis and Nancy to marry when she was gone.

As for Lewis, his great act of kindness was to finish this house, the Nauvoo House, which Joseph had started. Lewis, of course, scaled back Joseph's footprint, but Emma took delight in her upper bedroom window, which looked out to where the river bent away to the south. Emma often took her canoe, paddling out on the Mississippi. She was an accomplished canoeist, having grown up on the banks of the Susquehanna River in Pennsylvania. In her later years, Emma would sit near the window in her rocker and gaze out at the Mississippi River for hours. It fed her soul.

Sometime before Lewis completed Nauvoo House, Emma's youngest son, David—then in his twenties, but not yet mad—painted *Bend in the River*, a view from the bluffs downstream. In the foreground, atop the bluffs, a family enjoys a picnic. Overhead spreads a vast sky of dark, broken clouds, suffused with the glow of a sun already set. At the center of this vista stand the brick walls of the unfinished Nauvoo House, the Smith homestead, the famous red store, and some abandoned houses upstream. And drawing all elements together is the serene reflection of the river as it bends around the Nauvoo point.

10

Back in Saint Paul, I sit at my own south-facing window above the Mississippi River, contemplating the powerful, contrasting feelings I experienced in Nauvoo. What I felt

was a spiritual tension, having little to do with the theocratic divide that split the church after Joseph Smith's death
(and that may have contributed to David Smith's loss of
mental health). That theocratic divide does persist in Nauvoo—in spite of an ongoing rapprochement between the two
churches; you'll see it in the differing emphases of the two
visitor's centers, and in the conspicuous contrast between
the one church's proselytizing and the other's restraint
from proselytizing.

As an outsider, I have no particular interest in whether
Joseph Smith's prophetic mantle fell to Brigham Young or to
his son Joseph Smith III. It's the life of the spirit that interests
me, and Nauvoo has become for me a spiritual topography for
sorting through conflicting yearnings. In symbolic terms, the
great bend in the river can be a threshold to adventure, or an
enclosure of acceptance. Do I cross the river and take to the trail
(wherever that may lead) or dwell beside the river and put down
roots? Am I driven by feelings of desolation or drawn by feelings
of consolation?

These terms, *consolation* and *desolation*, were used by Ignatius of Loyola to describe two kinds of powerful feelings that
can direct our lives. Ignatius developed his *Spiritual Exercises*
in the 1520s as a guide for spiritual direction, to enable one to
discern God's presence in one's life and to make choices that
lead to a deeper inner vitality. Feelings of *desolation* lead one
away from that deepening life, and feelings of *consolation* lead
one toward a deepening life. What Nauvoo has done for me
is to make those feelings visible, providing a topography for
contemplating my inner life and to discern what is right for my
soul at this time.

For me, the three houses of Emma—that constellation of buildings at the bottom of the bend—evoke deep feelings of consolation. Emma turned from the church in her time of desolation. She told a visitor to Nauvoo in 1856: "I have always avoided talking to my children about having anything to do in the church, for I have suffered so much I have dreaded to have them take any part in it."

When others pursued the "exodus to greatness," Emma turned toward the common—attending to her property, taking pride in her children's development, and in practicing hospitality. After twenty or more years of marriage to Lewis, Emma wrote to her son Joseph III: "I often find I have to yield my will to surrounding circumstances, so I am daily trying to learn St. Paul's lesson . . . to be contented with our *condition*, to pray always, and in *all things* to give thanks."

Early in her forty-year Nauvoo sojourn, well before Joseph was murdered, Emma seems already to have been moving to a more grounded life of the spirit. In a recent study of the two Mormon hymnals Emma compiled, Rachel Cope, a BYU church historian, makes this observation: "While Smith's first hymnal [of 1835] highlights the emphasis she and other early Mormons placed on immediately establishing a city of Zion . . . her second hymnal [of 1841] underscores the need to develop and foster a personal relationship with a gracious and merciful Saviour."

As I near the end of my professional career, mediating feelings of desolation stirred up by a world I now barely recognize, I rejoice in the consolation I experienced in Nauvoo. I wonder how my life would be different had I encountered a Nauvoo in my youth. As a teacher of young people, I grow more keenly interested in considering their view of the world. Many of Nauvoo's early visitors were young—Thomas Kane, Charlotte Haven, and Frederick Piercy, all in their early twenties when they came to Nauvoo and pondered the landscape they found here. I want to add one more youthful perspective that captures, for me, all the enchantment I have felt in Nauvoo. In doing so, I imagine my younger self contemplating the older self I have become.

Julius Chambers was a twenty-two-year-old Cornell grad when he set out in 1872 on a canoe journey down the Mississippi River, from Lake Itasca to the Gulf. Chambers would become a great journalist and travel writer, and published a book when he was sixty, called *The Mississippi River and Its Wonderful Valley: Twenty-Seven Hundred and Seventy-Five Miles from Source to Sea*. A few years before then, he looked back on his youthful visit to Nauvoo in this sketch from the *Brooklyn Daily Eagle* of 1907. By this time, Emma was long dead, but his memory of her was vivid:

> In the summer of 1872, I was paddling down the Mississippi in a canoe, built for the trip at Troy, NY. At the nightfall of a July evening, after a long day's work, I saw on the Illinois shore, upon a fine bluff, a red brick building that indicated a town of more than village size. Making a landing, I climbed to the top of the plateau and learned that the building that had attracted my attention was the only hotel in the place. What was much more important, I was told the town was Nauvoo . . .
>
> When I applied at the office for supper I was received by an elderly woman. My eye-memory of the face and the figure of the distinguished old lady is quite distinct. She was tall, for her sex; her hair was gray, not white, and was combed straight

over her temples. Her face was thin; her nose lean, aquiline and pointed. Her mouth was small; her chin was badly shaped and protruded; her eyes were very noticeable, although their color cannot be recalled. They were gray or blue, in all likelihood. I also remember her hands, which were small and had well cared for nails. Of course, all these characteristics were not noticed the first meeting, but were the result of studious observation that evening and during an hour passed in her interesting company next morning—because I remained at Nauvoo for the night.

We talked long into the evening, for this aged woman appeared glad to see even a boy from the great East . . . She appeared to know very little about the literature of the time and to care nothing about it. I remember she had read several of Dickens' novels. But her waking hours were largely passed seated in a tall-backed rocking-chair, near the edge of the bluff, with her eyes fixed upon the majestic Mississippi before her; after darkness fell she turned her vision down the river toward the flickering lights of Keokuk, on the Iowa shore.

She was a picture of a fine woman, stranded on the ice-shore of age, amid surroundings with which she was entirely out of sympathy and among people who did not appreciate her intellect or her innate refinement . . .

My last sight of this venerable woman occurred next forenoon as she stood upon the bluff in front of the red hotel and waved her hand when I headed for the center of the broad stream to get into deep water on the Keokuk rapids . . .

Whenever a desolation of spirit comes creeping upon me, and I find myself out of sympathy with the people and prevailing culture, I hold on to this vision of Emma "with her eyes fixed upon the majestic Mississippi before her." Emma's forty-year sojourn speaks to my soul; her rootedness—embracing the river, dwelling within its great, encompassing arc—has made this ground sacred. Her life represents a counter to so much of the forward-looking movement of American religious and cultural values. The way of the river is not the way of the trail, and I want to live fully, in my time and in my place, as Emma lived in hers.

BLUFFS

Stalking the Sacred

These bluffs that plod upriver
like a caravan of camels are tricksters, working
their high magic on me, luring my eyes
down, sometimes even
below the water line, to discover
those soundings of
deeper truths.

—"BLUFFING" BY DICK STAHL

1

FOR THE LAST FOUR YEARS, I'VE MADE A PILGRIMAGE IN early autumn down to Effigy Mounds, a national monument in northeastern Iowa, rising high above the Mississippi and Yellow Rivers. The Yellow River is an exquisite stream, with rainbow and brown trout and smallmouth bass. It emerges from the woods near Effigy Mounds, then slips into the Mississippi, concealed by a pedestrian bridge, the highway, and a railroad bridge. The monument, too, is somewhat obscured, and travelers can drive right past it, unaware. Autumn is the best time to stop and enter the forest, long sacred to the Ho-Chunk and to their ancestors and to other indigenous people.

In the visitor's center, you can learn about the early builders of the mounds—there are some two hundred mounds around here—and ponder their purpose, the meaning of the shapes of birds and bears, and their orientation along the bluff top. You can walk the trail all the way to the top, passing by a variety of mysterious, ancient forms.

The first ascent to Eagle Rock and Fire Point is gentle and well traveled. Here the trail is wide, cushioned with wood chips and gentle switchbacks. Fire Point Mound, I'm told, contains burnt clay that was carried up from the Mississippi River, a thousand years ago or more. Through the open woods, I imagine a slow procession of silent figures carrying baskets of river mud up the switchback trails. The stillness feels as I imagine Lothlórien to be, Tolkien's elvish world, where ancient things live on.

On the second and third ascents—to the Twin Views and Third Scenic View—the wood chips give way to gravel and grass, and the trail takes you past the Great Bear group of effigies. These sites provide long vistas, upstream and downstream.

The final ascent is longer, traversing deep ravines and bending in a wide loop through the forest. Here the trail is rocky, eroded from periodic rains, and strewn with the thick, burst husks of the shagbark hickory. There are some scattered acorns, too, but mostly hickory husks. I hear the high-pitched sounds of nearby chipmunks, as regular as dripping faucets. Few visitors seem to come this far, but the solitude rewards the effort.

I am grateful to walk so deep into this forest. Thoughts I carried with me start to fall away, and I become mindful only of the space around. The red oaks and aspens, and even the maples, seem very tall here, reaching for the sky. Splashes of color edge the trail—goldenrod, little blue asters, jewelweed.

Then the trail climbs up from a deep ravine and, at the crest, turns back, and all at once, glistening through the trees, is the Mississippi River, stretching out far below. The trail passes a row of seven conical mounds, dips back down, then ends atop a limestone outcropping. This is Hanging Rock. Instinctively, I pause, then step down to a natural seat of stone, framed by several gnarled cedars. It's like a private box seat, high above the stage of nature. I stand at the precipice and look across the forest canopy, some four hundred feet or so above the Mississippi River.

A steady breeze sweeps up from the south, bending the grasses at the edge of the bluff. A fence has been installed for safety. I sit in the royal seat of stone and listen to the wind. It is wordless and insistent. I study the gnarled cedars that cling tenaciously to the rocks; they are the only conifers I've seen on my walk to Hanging Rock. Here, too, are several chinquapin oaks with their large, toothed leaves. Once used for railroad ties, fences, and fuel, few of these hardy oaks remain. Intolerant of shade, they are a unique feature of Mississippi River bluffs, and rarely are they found anywhere else.

Like the rarity of these chinquapin oaks, there's an elusive presence I have felt here, and nowhere else. On one of my early visits to Effigy Mounds, with a weighty decision on my mind and no clarity of insight on how to make it, I felt encompassed here, at Hanging Rock, by a tranquility of spirit, as if the question I could not answer already had been answered.

Having come to this overlook for several years now, I want to know more about what that presence might be—so difficult to name, yet numinous, transcendent. So I sit on the stone among the cedars, and open myself to the vast expanse of landscape, and to the thoughts coursing through me. I wonder, what makes this, or any landscape, sacred? Is it sacred only for those with ancestral visionaries? Do the seven ancient mounds behind me make this sacred? Is sacredness selective?

N. Scott Momaday, an elderly Kiowa writer, has much to say about the sacred. "To encounter the sacred is to be alive at the deepest center of human existence," he writes. Rainy Mountain is his sacred site, and there are others that he names "At Devils Tower or Canyon de Chelly or the Cahokia Mounds, you touch the pulse of the living planet; you feel its breath upon you. You become one with a spirit that pervades geologic time and space."

I learned from Momaday that sacred sites can be *made* sacred—consecrated, by blood, by sacrifice, by experience and story. What sets this bluff apart from other scenic bluffs? Do the ancient mounds embody human acts of sacrifice and story—of river mud carried up the trails, basketful by basketful, to recognize and celebrate the spirit that pervades both time and space?

2

Back home in Minnesota, on the east side of Saint Paul, the Indian Mounds Regional Park preserves half a dozen ancient mounds on the bluff high above the river. Once there were dozens; six mounds remain, enclosed by iron fences extending to the bluff's edge.

I love biking to this park on the bluff and pausing by the mounds to gaze out across the wide plain below. Union Pacific and Canadian Pacific trains are coupling and uncoupling their cars in the switchyard. Empty barges lie moored at the river's bend. Small planes drop down onto the flat expanse of Holman Field. Between the switchyard and the airfield, beside the shallow waters of Pig's Eye Lake, the city discharges wastewater from several million inhabitants. If you look closely—past the transport and storage facilities—you'll see a narrow stretch of parkland on the river's west bank. This is Kaposia Landing, once the site of a Dakota summer village, now an open recreation space. To the west is the downtown skyline of Saint Paul. It's a lot to take in!

Most come for the scenery, few for the sacred. Last summer, when the city of Saint Paul pulled back the park's trails from the edge of the bluff to preserve the sanctity of these mounds, there was an outcry from some who felt deprived of the scenery. But ample space still remains for scenic overlooks, and both the scenic and the sacred are maintained.

Mounds like these were found all along the river's bluffs, from here on down to the ancient city of Cahokia, near present-day Saint Louis, and all along the Ohio, and other rivers—mounds raised a thousand years ago by people who long since have disappeared. The upper Mississippi River is ancient land, built over millions of years from the accumulated deposits of vast inland seas. When the last glaciers retreated some twelve thousand years ago, a mighty river of meltwater carved out the bluffs. Glaciers that had scoured the lands to the east and the lands to the west, inexplicably left this eight-hundred-mile stretch along the upper Mississippi untouched by glacial debris, or drift. Hence, the term Driftless Area. Here, the vistas astonish, and a vast geological record, embedded in the layers of limestone, shale, and sandstone, provokes thoughts of time and eternity.

As I read through guidebooks and narratives, the word *enchanting* keeps showing up to describe the upper Mississippi River bluffs. It's an old word, and resonant, derived from the Latin, *incantare*, a magic spell, or incantation. It also suggests singing—*cantare* means "to sing"—as in *cantor*, *cantata*, or *chant*.

Unfortunately, like *awesome*, the word *enchanting* has been diminished by overuse and misuse. So, when Mark Twain came back to the Mississippi River in 1882—by then a world-famous author, known for his humor and sarcasm—he wrote deliberately, "We move up the river—always through enchanting

scenery, there being no other kind on the Upper Mississippi."
The word *enchant* shows up frequently in *Life on the Mississippi*,
but usually with a somewhat satirical inflection. One chapter is
called "Enchantments and Enchanters." In another, Twain lam-
poons a garrulous passenger who boards the steamboat at La
Crosse, gushing on and on about the "enchanting landscape":

> What grander river scenery can be conceived, as we gaze upon
> this enchanting landscape, from the uppermost point of these
> bluffs upon the valleys below? The primeval wildness and awful
> loneliness of these sublime creations of nature and nature's God,
> excite feelings of unbounded admiration, and the recollection of
> which can never be effaced from the memory.

But speaking more directly, Twain's own description of the
bluffs is rich and without effusion:

> The majestic bluffs that overlook the river, along through this
> region, charm one with the grace and variety of their forms and
> the soft beauty of their adornment. The steep verdant slope,
> whose base is at the water's edge, is topped by a lofty rampart of
> broken, turreted rocks, which are exquisitely rich and mellow in
> color—mainly dark browns and dull greens, but splashed with
> other tints. And then you have the shining river, winding here
> and there and yonder . . . And it is all as tranquil and reposeful
> as dreamland and has nothing this-worldly about it—nothing to
> hang a fret or a worry upon.
>
> Until the unholy train comes tearing along—which it pres-
> ently does, ripping the sacred solitude to rags and tatters with
> its devil's warwhoop and the roar and thunder of its rushing
> wheels—and straightway you are back in this world.

I quote this passage at length, partly for its beauty, but more for its suggestion of a fabric of sacred solitude that is easily torn "to rags and tatters" by the demonic noise of an unholy train. Twain had a particular dislike for the river trains as they displaced the steamboats after the American Civil War. And today, trains still come tearing along between the river and the bluff— thundering carriers of the heartland's commerce.

3

I visit the river bluffs intentionally, starting with the overlooks. I'm caught by the scenic, and looking for something more. Above the town of Alma, on Buena Vista Bluff, a young couple stands near me. I'm looking out over Lock and Dam No. 4 and the miniature village below, with its ribbon of railroad. Their backs are to the scenery, their uplifted faces are smiling at his extended phone. He makes a few attempts at a selfie, then turns to me.

"Will you take our picture?" He gestures vaguely at the distance behind them. "With all of that?"

I step on a bench and move the frame around, trying to squeeze in the distant arrow of an approaching barge. "Awesome," he says, inspecting the tiny, framed image. She grins.

Atop the seven-hundred-foot Grandad Bluff outside La Crosse, a monument proclaims that Father James Lloyd Breck in 1850 brought a group of pioneer missionaries here one fine Sunday to celebrate the Eucharist. I wonder, was it merely an Easter spectacle that brought them here to worship, so high above the valley? Or was their climbing effort an act of worship in itself, a deliberate response to something they found holy, prompting them to raise a stone, like Jacob, and declare: "Surely God was in this place and I did not know it"? I do not know.

I walk the outdoor way of the cross that Father Michael Flammang built in 1861, and I pause at each of the fourteen stations—lovely, bricked alcoves strung along a path ascending the bluff behind St. Donatus Church. It's a few miles back from the river, opposite Galena.

"Be sure to go all the way up to the Pietà Chapel," the sister says as she hands me the accompanying readings. "It's as close to heaven as you will get." She smiles. "Until you die, of course."

On Brady's Bluff, in Perrot State Park, between Winona and La Crosse, I gaze upon the mysterious island, Trempealeau, the sacred "mountain whose foot is bathed in the river." A thousand years ago or so, indigenous Mississippians settled here and found it sacred, as have later indigenous peoples.

After the American Civil War, a disillusioned veteran and former chaplain to the Thirtieth Wisconsin Infantry sought solace in long walks along these bluffs, then sacred to the Ojibwe. The landscape appealed to his grieving, wounded soul, and he convinced himself that he had found the lost Garden of Eden. In 1886, he published an eccentric little book, *Found at Last: The Veritable Garden of Eden, or a Place that Answers the Bible Description of that Notable Spot Better Than Anything Yet Discovered.*

I crisscross the river frequently to find such vistas, delighting in their beauty, yet seeming always to bump into the religious. I'm not seeking the religious, or even religious ideas. There are excellent books on that subject, such as *Gods of the Mississippi*, with its stated objective "to explain how the physical and imagined features of the Mississippi contributed to the development of religious ideas and communities throughout American history." What I'm looking for is that fabric of sacred solitude, and it continues to elude me.

4

The late geographer Donald W. Meinig, author of *The Shaping of America: A Geographical Perspective on 500 Years of History*, has helped me understand how we make sense of a landscape. The central problem, Meinig explains, is that "any landscape is composed not only of what lies before our eyes but what lies within our heads." Meinig outlines ten ways we might compose a landscape.

The first is a romantic way of seeing "landscape as nature." Such a view is nostalgic, he says, stemming from a yearning for wildness. That nostalgia tempts us to remove human life from the scene, and visually, attempt to restore nature to a "pristine condition."

But such a perspective is itself a bluff. It can't be sustained. You have to "overlook" too much, like the unholy train. But while it lasts, the view from the bluffs can be intoxicating.

Meinig names nine more ways to see a landscape: as *habitat*, as *artifact*, as *system* (such as, an ecosystem), as *problem* (as in engineering or design), as *wealth*, as *ideology*, as *history*, as *place*, and as *aesthetic*. In my imagination, I try them all in various places. It's an exhilarating exercise in perception and enables me to practice what N. Scott Momaday had advised—to give oneself up to a particular landscape, to look at it from as many angles as possible, and wonder about it.

The *sacred* is not one of Meinig's ten ways of seeing. But on the bluffs of the upper Mississippi, the markers and mounds suggest that there have been those who experienced some kind of seeing in a sacred manner and marked the place.

When I explore a landscape, I am drawn to the edges—to a cliff, a ledge, a shoreline, a ridge or ravine. The edges, the fringes and boundaries of things, heighten my expectancy. Edge—the very word itself can transform an ordinary term—like *time* or *night* or *tomorrow*—into something stimulating to the imagination: "the edge of time" or "the edge of night" or "the edge of tomorrow." On the bluffs of the upper Mississippi, I stand on a threshold of space and time. Beneath me are the accumulated deposits of millions of years; and beyond, stretching from horizon to horizon, the inscrutable river.

5

I need some guides or mentors. So I enlist a trinity of muses to guide me on my quest—three men in a boat, as I think of them familiarly—three writers who made our waters mythic: pond, river, and sea. Their lives overlapped in the nineteenth century. All three were born with white male privilege; but that's not why I choose them. They are writers whose works have guided and inspired me, writers whose words I've come to trust. They have been my intellectual and creative mentors. None were religious, but each was perceptive—spiritually open and receptive to mystery. They understood the obligations of privilege and saw that the constructed divisions of race and class—and the injustices those divisions have inflicted—must be confronted by all of us. And they projected their voices and visions for a human community beyond those divides.

Henry Thoreau, Herman Melville, and Samuel Clemens came to the Mississippi River, each at a critical time in the course of their lives. I decided to visit the sites where each had stood, and imaginatively stare with them, beside the river, into time and place. If I caught no glimpse of eternity's disclosure, the journey alone would not be in vain. I'd surely learn something about their perspectives, these pilgrims who built no altars, raised no stones, but left a very long trail of words—and a few faint tracings of their presence along the river. These three would serve as my "stations of the bluffs."

6

I started with Henry as the most accessible. In the last full year of his too-short life, Henry came to Minnesota to improve his health. He hung around the Saint Anthony Falls and sauntered the streets of Minneapolis and Saint Paul. He visited Bdote and steamed up the Minnesota River to visit the Lower Sioux Agency. His footsteps were available to my footsteps and my imagination.

Henry had always loved rivers. At age twenty-one, he wrote in his newly begun journal:

> For the first time it occurred to me this afternoon what a piece of wonder a river is,—a huge volume of matter ceaselessly rolling through the fields and meadows of this substantial earth, making haste from the high places, by stable dwellings of men and Egyptian Pyramids, to its restless reservoir. One would think that, by a very natural impulse, the dwellers upon the headwaters of the Mississippi and Amazon would follow in the trail of their waters to see the end of the matter.
>
> (September 5, 1838)

In 1849, the year he published *A Week on the Concord and Merrimack Rivers*, Henry's imagination was stirred by the exhibitions in Boston of Champney's *Great Panoramic Picture of the River Rhine and Its Banks* and Stockwell's *Colossal Panorama of the Upper and Lower Mississippi Rivers*. About the panorama of the Rhine, Henry said, "I floated along under the spell of enchantment, as if I had been transported to an heroic age." But the Mississippi panorama brought thoughts "more of the future than of the past or present,—I saw that this was a Rhine stream of a different kind."

Henry didn't actually see the Mississippi River until that last year of his life. His first impressions were of the "great rafts of sawed lumber and of logs, twenty rods or more in length, by five or six wide, floating down, all from the pine region above the Falls."

"Time is but the stream I go a-fishing in," he famously said. But in 1861, time was becoming a bloody torrent; the nation was going to war. Henry was slowly dying from an incessant cough, and he had come to Minnesota with a young friend, Horace Mann Jr.

Meanwhile, a thousand miles downstream, Sam Clemens's years on the Mississippi had come to an abrupt and decisive end. He had realized his childhood ambition of becoming a Mississippi riverboat pilot, but the outbreak of war shut down commercial traffic and crushed his hopes "that I was going to follow the river the rest of my days and die at the wheel."

In Minnesota, young men from all around the state were responding enthusiastically to Lincoln's call for volunteers in April 1861; within two weeks, ten companies, a regiment of a thousand, had been formed. When Henry visited the bluffs of

Fort Snelling on May 29, he saw several hundred volunteers of the Minnesota First Infantry, drilling and waiting anxiously for their orders. Some companies had been posted at forts upstream.

After nearly a month of botanizing, sauntering, and reading in the Minneapolis libraries, Henry and Horace steamed up the Minnesota (St. Peter's) River to the Lower Sioux Agency where they joined a council of frustrated Dakota and listened to them speak. In his journal, Henry noted: "The Indians, as usual, having the advantage in point of truth and earnestness, and therefore of eloquence." This place of exile would be known as Cansa'yapi, "where they marked the trees red."

On Saturday, June 22, Henry and Horace came back to the Twin Cities, down the Minnesota River to where it joins the Mississippi, passing by Bdote and the bluffs of Fort Snelling around 9:00 p.m. Henry made notes in his journal of the many birds he sighted—spotted sandpiper, bank swallow, kingfisher, ducks, jays, Wilson's thrush, rose-breasted grosbeak, Maryland yellowthroat, whippoorwill, nighthawk, blue heron, mud hen, hawks, pigeons, white-bellied swallows, vireos . . . About the Minnesota River, he noted: "Clay-colored water yet pretty clear in a tumbler when settled."

Henry observed the confluence at Pike Island, but left no indication of whether it stirred his imagination. In *A Week on the Concord and Merrimack Rivers*, Henry told of passing "a large and densely wooded island," then musing:

> An island always pleases my imagination, even the smallest, as a small continent and integral portion of the globe . . . There is commonly such a one at the junction of two rivers, whose currents bring down and deposit their respective sands in the eddy

at their confluence, as it were the womb of a continent. By what
a delicate and far-stretched contribution every island is made!
What an enterprise of Nature thus to lay the foundations of and
to build up the future continent.

What happened that day near the bluffs of Fort Snelling,
rising above Bdote and Pike Island, was a confluence of historical and intellectual currents that actually would help "to lay the
foundations of and to build up the future continent." It stirs
me to deep contemplation. I imagine Henry David Thoreau,
still largely unknown, back from his long excursion up the
Minnesota River, returning in the wake of the Minnesota First,
which, only hours before, had departed down the Mississippi
aboard the *Northern Belle* and *War Eagle* for the long journey on
to Washington and into the great battles of the American Civil
War. None could have known the courses of their brief remaining lives, and even less how their individual actions would flow
into the larger currents of history, acquiring a significance and
immortality unimagined. Henry and Horace spent that Saturday night at the Merchants Hotel in Saint Paul, then caught the
next day's steamboat down to Red Wing.

One morning in mid-June, I drive to Red Wing to climb
up He Mni Can, more commonly known as Barn Bluff. I park
at the trailhead at the east end of the bluff and walk up a gentle
slope to a very long flight of stairs. Much of the bluff has been
quarried away. At the top, there are two overlooks, half a mile
apart; the east end looks out over the river, and the west end,
upstream, over the town. I avoid the narrow, rocky trail along
the north edge, nearest the river, remembering that several have
fallen to their deaths here in recent years.

I'm here because Henry stopped here on his way home from Minnesota. But I'm also drawn because this bluff has been sacred to Mdewakanton Dakota—and to others, much earlier, who raised burial mounds atop it.

When US Army major Stephen Harriman Long, the topographical engineer who sited Fort Snelling, climbed up here in 1819, he found "the sublime and beautiful here blended in a most enchanting manner." There it is again, that provocative word.

Henry and Horace climbed the bluff on Monday, June 24, 1861. They carried with them letters they had just received from Concord. On Wednesday, June 26, Henry wrote back to one, Franklin B. Sanborn, a member of the notorious Secret Six who had supported John Brown's failed raid on Harpers Ferry. Here are some passages from Thoreau's long, descriptive reply:

Redwing, Minnesota, June 26, 1861

Mr. Sanborn,—I was very glad to find awaiting me, on my arrival here on Sunday afternoon, a letter from you. I have performed this journey in a very dead and alive manner, but nothing has come so near waking me up as the receipt of letters from Concord. I read yours and one from my sister (and Horace Mann, his four), near the top of a remarkable isolated bluff here, called Barn Bluff, or the Grange, or Redwing Bluff, some four hundred and fifty feet high, and half a mile long,—a bit of the main bluff or bank standing alone . . .

I am not even so well informed as to the progress of the war as you suppose. I have seen but one Eastern paper (that, by the way, *was* the "Tribune") for five weeks. I have not taken much pains to get them; but, necessarily, I have not seen any paper at all for more than a week at a time. The people of Minnesota have *seemed* to me more cold,—to feel less implicated in this war than the people of Massachusetts . . .

I was glad to be told yesterday that there was a good deal of weeping here at Redwing the other day, when the volunteers stationed at Fort Snelling followed the regulars to the seat of the war . . .

The grand feature hereabouts is, of course, the Mississippi River. Too much can hardly be said of its grandeur, and of the beauty of this portion of it.

I imagine the transcendentalist of Walden Pond, sitting atop He Mni Can in the last summer of his life, reading letters from Concord above the Mississippi River, and contemplating Minnesota's entry into the war. It's an image that continues to move me, and it has stirred other pilgrims to visit this bluff.

"Too much can hardly be said of its grandeur," Henry wrote about the Mississippi River; but then, Henry did not go on in his letter to say anything at all about its grandeur and beauty! What he described, instead, was the earthiness and physicality of the muddy Minnesota River, recalling his recent trip upstream to Cansa'yapi, the Lower Sioux Agency:

In making a short turn, we repeatedly and designedly ran square into the steep and soft bank, taking in a cart-load of earth,—this being more effectual than the rudder to fetch us about again; or the deeper water was so narrow and close to the shore, that we were obliged to run into and break down at least fifty trees which overhung the water . . . I could pluck almost any plant on the bank from the boat. We very frequently got aground, and then drew ourselves along with a windlass and a cable fastened to a tree, or we swung round in the current, and completely blocked up and blockaded the river, one end of the boat resting on each shore.

That's the kind of enthusiasm Henry voiced in *The Maine Woods*: "Think of our life in nature—daily to be shown matter, to come in contact with it—rocks, trees, wind on our cheeks! the solid earth! the actual world! the common sense! Contact! Contact!"

It's his cartload of river mud, imaginatively brought to the top of He Mni Can (which, by the way, means "hill, water, wood"). In the second chapter of his most famous book, *Walden*, Henry wrote: "Let us settle ourselves, and work and wedge our feet downward through the mud and slush of opinion, and prejudice, and tradition, and delusion, and appearance . . . till we come to a hard bottom and rocks in place, which we can call reality, and say, This is, and no mistake."

For the first time, I'm starting to grasp the impulse to build an altar, to raise a marker, form a mound—not to mark some spiritual belief in reality transcended, or nature made pristine, but to honor the spiritual experience of the material, bringing river mud to the top, "that future ages might know."

"Be it life or death," Henry concluded that second chapter, "we crave only reality. If we are really dying, let us hear the rattle in our throats and feel cold in the extremities; if we are alive, let us go about our business."

The same day he wrote back to Franklin Sanborn, Henry left Red Wing on his journey home, boarding the very same *War Eagle* that just a few days earlier had borne away the men of the Minnesota First. Henry would never see another summer. Most of the Minnesota First would never again see home.

7

Farther down the stream of time, Galena, Illinois, was once the busiest port along the Mississippi River, midway between Saint Louis and Saint Paul. It is an exquisite town, hugging the hills and bluffs along the Galena River about three miles in from the Mississippi River.

"Have you noticed?" asks the tour guide who accompanies us on a trolley tour through the historic district of town. "See how many couples are holding hands?"

The town exudes a nineteenth-century kind of romance. Its houses and churches, constructed of Galena brick, have been preserved and restored, its history venerated and made accessible. Nearby Casper Bluff, overlooking the Mississippi River, is covered with ancient burial mounds and the great thunderbird effigy with a wingspan of more than one hundred feet.

Tourism sustains Galena today, but in 1840 it was lead. Galena was then the nation's leading producer of lead and would provide much of the material for the musket and minié balls that shattered hundreds of thousands of human limbs and made the American Civil War our nation's bloodiest.

Galena was home to Ulysses S. Grant and other Civil War generals. But in 1840, Grant was unknown and the Civil War as yet unimagined. In 1840, the Galena River was called the Fever River—about 350 feet wide and deep enough for eighteen steamboats to dock at once. In 1840, that one year alone, three hundred steamboats made stops in Galena and carried away twenty-two million pounds of lead.

In 1840, a young Herman Melville came to Galena to visit his uncle, Major Thomas Melvill. Herman Melville turned 21 that summer of 1840. (His family had added the *e* to their name some years earlier). As a teenager, Herman had worked on his uncle's farm back in Pittsfield, Massachusetts, and apparently adored him. Years later, when Herman wrote *Moby-Dick* on that same Pittsfield farm, he used as his writing desk "an old thing of my Uncle the Major's" which had been "packed away."

We don't know very much about Herman's 1840 visit. The only statement we have is from an unpublished sketch he wrote later, now housed in the archives of the New York Public Library: "I visited my now venerable kinsman in his western home, and was anew struck by the contrast between the man and his environment." That's it. All other evidence comes from external sources. No journal entries. No extant letters. Only that singular statement.

Herman did not say what that contrast was that struck him concerning "the man and his environment," but whatever it was, it stayed with him. That one poignant sentence projected a theme that would inform all of his writing, especially *Moby-Dick*; and it continues to strike readers of that great novel today—the contrast between "man and his environment." One literary scholar, Merton M. Sealts Jr., has tracked "the ghost of Major Melvill" in the guise of various characters throughout Herman's writing, including his last, unfinished novel, *Billy Budd*.

The environment of Galena is a fascinating subject in itself, as is the story of Herman's "venerable kinsman." So much room for the imagination to play!

Herman's uncle moved to Galena around 1838, encouraged by a Captain Hezekiah Gear. Now Captain Gear made a fortune in Galena, mining lead. But exactly what transpired between Thomas Melvill and Hezekiah Gear is altogether murky. Historical records show that Thomas Melvill became an influential civil servant and served on a number of commissions. Gear's daughter, Clarissa, said that her father, Captain Gear, hired Thomas as his business manager, but Thomas had betrayed that trust, embezzling from Gear. When confronted by Gear, she said Thomas had confessed the money was all spent, and that her father then told the old major: "I could send you to prison for life, but that would not bring back the money. Major, for the sake of your good family and for the sake of your gray hair, I'll not punish you, but I never want to lay eyes on you again."

Herman didn't stay long in Galena. I can't help but wonder what forces redirected the arc of his life, hurling him back to New Bedford and on, out to sea. What was that intense contrast he perceived that summer of his twenty-first year? Could it be the contrast between Galena's prosperity and his uncle's penury? Or did he perceive a much larger incongruity between his uncle's pursuits and the natural environment of Galena? Could young Herman foresee the devastating environmental consequence of deforesting the bluffs?

Around Galena, wood was used for smelting lead and for refueling steamboats. And as the trees disappeared, the land, made barren, soon eroded and the river silted in. What flows through Galena today is little more than a creek and is prone to flooding; but the ghostly outline of its original magnificence clearly can be seen.

Herman left Galena before summer's end. Likely, he went upstream to the Falls of Saint Anthony, says biographer Hershel Parker; then he came back down the river to Cairo and up the

Ohio River. Herman's steamboat would have passed the sleepy
town of Hannibal, where four-year-old Sam Clemens and his
parents had just settled into their new home. By November, Herman was back in New York, and a few weeks later, he boarded
the whaling ship *Acushnet*, bound for Cape Horn and the remote
islands of the South Pacific.

Pamela has come to Galena with me, having recently become
my wife and dearest companion. We walk hand in hand through
the streets, spending far too much money in antique shops, lingering over lunch in the market house café, and later sipping
cocktails in the Generals' Restaurant lounge. We are reluctant to
leave, suspended in time. We stay in the historic DeSoto House
Hotel, named for the first European to see the Mississippi River.
All the rooms are named for famous people who have stayed
here. Robert E. Lee came up from Saint Louis in July of 1859,
working as a lieutenant on upper Mississippi projects. Sam
Clemens, in January of 1869, spoke at the Methodist Episcopal
church, where Grant occasionally worshipped. Frederick Doug-
lass, in October 1854, gave the first anti-slavery speech in Galena
at the county courthouse. Elizabeth Cady Stanton joined Susan
B. Anthony on March 2, 1869, at Davis Hall to speak about
suffrage, and Anthony returned for a second visit two years later.
Theodore Roosevelt came on April 27, 1900, to celebrate Grant's
birthday; Stephen Douglas, in 1838, '52, '54, and '57, mostly to
criticize Lincoln, it seems.

On our last day in Galena, we drive out to Casper Bluff.
It's not likely Herman Melville would have seen it, for it is several miles south of Galena and somewhat difficult to find. We
drive out North Blackjack Road to Pilot Knob Road, then over
a narrow, deeply eroded dirt lane that seemed almost washed out

from the previous night's thunderstorm. When we arrive at the edge of the bluff, there are no people in sight.

Eagles are soaring high above the Harris Slough that spreads along the Mississippi River. For a few minutes, we gaze in silence at the vista. But we have come to see the thunderbird, and there are signs pointing the way. It's an awesome effigy. Its rounded shape and enormous wingspread are readily discernable against the earth and have endured in this place a thousand years or more.

We walk around the thunderbird in wordless wonder. This great, mythical being, a symbol of power for the Ho-Chunk, the Ojibwe, and indigenous nations all across this continent. There is one sign nearby describing the upper, middle, and lower cosmography of Woodland peoples. In some myths, the thunderbirds do battle with underwater spirits. I can't help but think of the great white whale that Herman's imagination created for his own symbolic tale.

So, what was the essence of Herman's brief trip to Galena? Had he caught from its bluffs some power that would fling him back east and on out to sea? Were seeds planted here of what would in time become the "mighty theme" of *Moby-Dick*? Did the incongruity of his uncle's situation inspire the tensions and motivations of his characters—Ishmael, Ahab, Bartleby, and Starbuck? I can only imagine. The worlds of Herman's novels are informed with tremendous tensions—intense pushing and pulling, heaving and hauling—between characters (like Ahab and Ishmael) and even within the souls of the characters themselves. In the mad pursuits of Ahab and of Ishmael, and in the world through which they journey, there are always enormous, mythic contrasts: "Consider them both, the sea and the land," Herman wrote in *Moby-Dick*, "and do you not find a strange analogy to something in yourself?"

Eventually, Herman returned imaginatively to the Mississippi River in *The Confidence-Man*, his last full-length novel, which follows a group of travelers on a steamboat. He wrote, almost breathlessly: "The sky slides into blue, the bluffs into bloom; the rapid Mississippi expands; runs sparkling and gurgling, all over in eddies; one magnified wake of a seventy-four. The sun comes out, a golden hussar, from his tent, flashing his helm on the world. All things, warmed in the landscape, leap."

8

I prepare for my third and final station, feeling a bit like Ebenezer Scrooge at the arrival of the third spirit—"Lead on." My expectations are not high. I am hoping to follow the traces of Sam Clemens, the person, and not Mark Twain, the mythmaker of the Mississippi.

I arrive in Hannibal, Missouri, on a glorious Saturday morning, standing with a languorous crowd before Tom Sawyer's old board fence. I have paid my respects to the Samuel Clemens childhood home and the Becky Thatcher home, and now stand indolently in the imagined place where Tom appears with a bucket of whitewash and a long-handled brush. It's an iconic image, popularized by Norman Rockwell and reproduced on a US postage stamp.

I hoped I would feel like a pilgrim in this celebrated place but instead feel detached. I saunter through the streets, hoping for something of Sam's spirit to catch me. Somewhere, I sit down and idly skim a copy of *The Adventures of Tom Sawyer* I had impulsively bought in the gift shop. Chapter 2 of that book begins:

> Saturday morning was come, and all the summer world was bright and fresh, and brimming with life. There was a song in every heart; and if the heart was young, the music issued at the lips. There was cheer in every face and a spring in every step. The locust-trees were in bloom, and the fragrance of the blossoms filled the air. Cardiff Hill, beyond the village and above it, was green with vegetation and it lay just far enough away to seem a Delectable Land, dreamy, reposeful, and inviting.

Cardiff Hill, I see, is just far enough away, at the north end of Main Street; so I decide to walk to it. A century ago, readers would have caught the allusion to "a Delectable Land" from John Bunyan's *Pilgrim's Progress*, where weary pilgrims catch their first glimpse of the Celestial City. Before Mark Twain made the hill famous, folks in old Hannibal would have known Cardiff Hill as Holliday's Hill.

But when I get to Cardiff Hill, nothing seems delectable or reposeful about it. At its base stands a sculpture of Tom Sawyer and Huck Finn, and behind it, a daunting flight of 244 steps leads up the hill to a lighthouse, built in 1935 to honor the centennial of Sam Clemens's birth.

The vegetation on the hill has grown thick. Cardiff Hill feels just like another neglected shrine. I study the locked door to the lighthouse. My guidebook informs me the lighthouse was dedicated and lighted by President Franklin D. Roosevelt in 1935, again by President Kennedy in 1963, and a third time by President Clinton.

I turn and look across the town spread out below, and over to the river. It doesn't take much effort to imagine all the cars and all the billboards are gone, and the sleepy little town of a century ago. There would be steamboats in place of barges on the glistening river. Downstream, on the other side of town, the bluff of Lover's Leap rises high, facing a string of islands. It's impossible not to think of time.

Sam Clemens climbed this hill, early one Sunday morning in the spring of 1882. He was world famous by then, in his mid-forties, and had come back to see the river he had left in 1861. "Twenty-one slow-drifting years that have come and gone since I last looked from the windows of a pilot-house," he says in *Life on the Mississippi*. During those twenty-one years, the Civil War had passed, Reconstruction had been abandoned, and the machinery of the Gilded Age was grinding westward. Sam, in that time, had pursued fame and fortune, mining silver in Nevada and gold in California. He'd been a reporter in San Francisco, a correspondent in Hawaii, and a traveling lecturer. Finally, as he puts it, "I became a scribbler of books." By 1882, Sam's books were many—among them, *Innocents Abroad*, *Roughing It*, and *The Adventures of Tom Sawyer*.

But the reviews of *The Prince and the Pauper* had been devastating, and the manuscript of what would become his greatest, *The Adventures of Huckleberry Finn*, lay unfinished. Financial and legal problems dogged him. His publisher wanted him to expand the popular *Atlantic Monthly* sketches "Old Times on the Mississippi" into a full-length book, *Life on the Mississippi*. Sam Clemens needed re-enchantment.

"After twenty-one years absence," he continues, "I felt a very strong desire to see the river again." Sam seems haunted by that interval of twenty-one years; he refers to it often: "A glory that once was had dissolved and vanished away in these twenty-one years." And again, "It is the blight of the war. Twenty-one years ago everything was trim and trig and bright."

This journey of 1882 would be his last trip on the river and, according to biographer Ron Powers, "the most essential sojourn of his creative life." Sam arrived in Saint Louis in April and was immediately disillusioned: "Half a dozen sound-asleep steamboats where I used to see a solid mile of wide-awake ones! This was melancholy, this was woeful . . . The towboat and the railroad had done their work, and done it well and completely." Sam went down the river to New Orleans, turned around, and came back upstream to Hannibal.

"The river is so thoroughly changed that I can't bring it back to mind even when the changes have been pointed out to me. It is like a man pointing out to me a place in the sky where a cloud has been," he writes. Towns and islands had vanished, swept away by the river. "The romance of boating is gone," he laments. "In Hannibal the steamboatman is no longer a god. The youth don't talk river slang anymore."

But early that Sunday morning, at the top of the hill, Sam looks out on the still-sleeping town and begins to think. At first, he feels like a boy again; but soon "my reflections spoiled all that," he says. It was a moment of quiet, but profound, transformation; and Sam describes that moment in *Life on the Mississippi*.

> From this vantage ground the extensive view up and down the river, and wide over the wooded expanses of Illinois, is very beautiful—one of the most beautiful on the Mississippi, I think; which is a hazardous remark to make, for the eight hundred

miles of river between St. Louis and St. Paul afford an unbroken succession of lovely pictures. It may be that my affection for the one in question biases my judgment in its favor; I cannot say as to that. No matter, it was satisfyingly beautiful to me, and it had this advantage over all the other friends whom I was about to greet again: it had suffered no change; it was as young and fresh and comely and gracious as ever it had been; whereas, the faces of the others would be old, and scarred with the campaigns of life, and marked with their griefs and defeats, and would give me no upliftings of spirit.

Scholars of "Mark Twain" have noticed the impact that river trip made on Sam's subsequent writing. Matt Klauza, for one, sees this moment of reflection at the top of Cardiff Hill as the turning point in Sam's writing. "His juxtaposition here between the eternally youthful river and the mortal town of his youth was a permanent sentiment," Klauza says; "from this point forward his writings about the Mississippi River would change in tone." Sam's writing grew darker, more insistently realistic. And his greatest book of all—which he resumed after this trip—confronts, with a disarming directness, the realities of racism in these United States.

I want to pause to consider this contemplative moment atop Cardiff Hill, even as I ponder my own thoughts about time, looking out on the river. Climbing the hill, Sam had wanted the illusion—to see the town as it had been and not as it was, to feel like the carefree boy in a straw hat, to believe things really had not changed very much. But his journey, from Saint Louis to New Orleans and back up to Hannibal, only deepened his sense of loss as he witnessed, not only the changes brought by time, but also the nation's appalling failure to African Americans after the Civil War.

So, it's quite understandable that Sam wants "to get a comprehensive view," as he puts it, to regain a perspective that would uplift his spirits and reassure him. But the view leads him into a moment of contemplation, and the illusion cannot be sustained.

Moments of contemplation like this don't come to us easily, says sociologist Parker Palmer. We prefer our illusions—both those personal illusions about ourselves and our world that keep us going from day to day, and those social illusions that keep systems of inequity and injustice in place. We live in a world that encourages illusion. "This is why the contemplative moment, the moment when illusion is stripped away and reality is revealed, is so hard to come by," Palmer says. "There is a vast conspiracy against it."

What I think Sam experienced that Sunday morning on the bluff above Hannibal was nothing less than sacred. The view, he says, was "satisfyingly beautiful." That river, which had seemed to him "so thoroughly changed," really "had suffered no change; it was as young and fresh and comely and gracious as ever it had been." The river endures, whereas the people, with all their griefs and defeats, offer no uplift to his spirit.

T. S. Eliot, the Nobel Prize–winning poet who grew up in Saint Louis, said that what made *The Adventures of Huckleberry Finn* so great was the river itself. It's the river that takes these two unlikely companions—a runaway white child of an alcoholic, and a black man fleeing slavery—not toward the freedom they imagine but deeper into danger, into conflict, and into the inner recesses of the heart and soul. Eliot called the river a god.

The characters Sam created in that book, and set adrift on a raft, set out with their own, separate illusions of freedom. And

for many chapters, drifting on the river seems to be the fulfill-
ment of blissful, unrestrained freedom! "You feel mighty free
and easy and comfortable on a raft," says Huck. But the river
has them in its grip and requires them to confront realities of
being human. When they drift past a field of watermelon, they
debate the ethics of stealing. When dangerous characters thrust
themselves onto the safety of the raft, there is always the problem
of lying and deception to deal with.

The river provides them with time for deep conversation,
too. "It's lovely to live on a raft. We had the sky up there, all
speckled with stars, and we used to lay on our backs and look up
at them, and discuss about whether they was made or only just
happened."

But as the journey continues, Huck's conscience gets to
grinding him. For as he has matured, and gained a sense of
responsibility to Jim, he recognizes he also has a communal
responsibility. And the laws of his community, and the religious
system he has inherited, tells him that slavery is justified, that
Jim is property, and that he, Huck, is a thief. So Huck embraces
another illusion of goodness and morality, and decides to get
right with God and clear his conscience. Driven by his illusion
of doing the right thing, he writes a letter to Jim's owner, Miss
Watson, to tell her where she can find her "property." He says:

> I felt good and all washed clean of sin for the first time I had ever
> felt so in my life, and I knowed I could pray now. But I didn't do
> it straight off, but laid the paper down and set there thinking—
> thinking how good it was all this happened so, and how near
> I come to being lost and going to hell. And went on thinking.
> And got to thinking over our trip down the river.

It's truly awesome to see a young person really thinking for themselves. To lay down the paper and begin to think—*really think*—through one's experience on the river of life. In Sam's novel, when Huck puts down the letter that is fueled by all the personal, social, and religious illusions he has carried, he accepts the reality of the contemplative moment. And as he thinks about the shared experiences on the river—the adventures, and dangers, and joys, and anxieties, and mutual support, and affection, and friendship—the illusions can't be sustained.

> I took [the letter] up, and held it in my hand. I was a-trembling, because I'd got to decide, forever, betwixt two things, and I knowed it. I studied a minute, sort of holding my breath, and then says to myself:
> "All right, then, I'll go to hell"—and tore it up.
> It was awful thoughts and awful words, but they was said. And I let them stay said; and never thought no more about reforming.

Huck embraces the contemplative moment offered by the river, but it requires moral courage. As Parker Palmer teaches, "The contemplative journey from illusion to reality may have peace as its destination, but en route it usually passes through some fearsome places."

9

Back home at my desk, I spread out my notes and considered the full journey, from bluff top to bluff top—from He Mni Can to Casper Bluff to Cardiff Hill—and the countless number of mounds that still mark the river's bluff tops, from Indian Mounds Regional Park to ancient Cahokia.

I observed this remarkable coincidence. Having noticed that the number twenty-one appeared frequently in my notes, I thought to connect them, and found, to my surprise, that the visits of my three muses to the Mississippi River occurred exactly twenty-one years apart—1840, 1861, and 1882. Furthermore, these equally spaced visits, both in time and topography, represent three stages in life when most of us seem vulnerable to time's stirring of consciousness—in the last years of life's journey, in the setting out on that journey, and at the midpoint, when disillusionment is keenest. Like Henry at Walden, with ruler in hand as he studied the map of the pond's soundings in winter, I wondered if this remarkable coincidence might extend into my life, here in the twenty-first year of the twenty-first century?

Fragments and phrases began clumping, like molecules cohering: *We crave only reality. A cartload of earth. Consider them both. The contrast between the man and his environment. No matter, it was satisfyingly beautiful. This is, and make no mistake!* The landscape infused with words of these enchanters of waters—of pond, river, and sea—the particle, wave, and field of the imaginative life—in all their manifold inflections—surface, flow, and depth—the river's upper, middle, and lower layers.

To be fully aware of being in time, of kairos more than chronos, present to the river's presence, yielding to its many confluences and bends, gorges, and bluffs. These patterns, rhythms, and recognitions speak to my soul—the stuff of myth in the making. Is this the sacred that I glimpse, impelling some to carry cartloads of mud to the top of the bluff, to build an altar, or to construct a tribute in words, as I have done? No matter, to me it is satisfyingly beautiful!

FIELD
Kaposia Landing

To think that the rivers will flow, and the snow
    fall, and fruits ripen,
and act upon others as upon us now—yet not
    act upon us!

—"To Think of Time" by Walt Whitman

T HERE IS A FIELD IN SOUTH SAINT PAUL, BETWEEN THE river and the railroad. Barges moor at the river's edge; and on the western side, freighted trains move slowly, north and south. The field itself is long and flat with ample room for baseball fields, walking trails, a dog park. Behind the railroad rise the bluffs of South Saint Paul; and to the distant north, above the trees, you'll glimpse the top of Saint Paul's skyline and the bluffs of Indian Mounds.

Light planes fly over, rising from Fleming Field to the south, or descending on Holman Field to the north. Eagles circle high overhead. There is—with all the unhurried movement around it—the stillness of sanctuary. This is Kaposia Landing.

The Mississippi River Trail runs through this field. Going north, it passes through a stretch of woods and along the edge of Holman Field and on, into the city of Saint Paul. Going south, the trail picks up the levee, where the Union Stockyards stood for many years. Farther south, the trail moves back, away from the river to follow the highway for several miles past houses and fields.

Several miles south, at Spring Lake Park, the trail begins to climb through prairies and forests and over deep ravines on former railway trestles. At the top is Schaar's Bluff, with its magnificent views above the islands and channels of Spring Lake, where the Mississippi River is very wide. Picnic grounds sprawl over the bluff top. Down from Schaar's Bluff, you'll practically coast your way to Lock and Dam No. 2 at the north edge of Hastings. Biking on this marvelous route feels more like a pilgrimage to me than a workout.

In South Saint Paul, I pause on the levee and begin to think. The very word *levee* is itself magic. As a child learning piano on the high plains of Wyoming, I was caught by the song "On the Levee," the last piece in book B. Out in that land of dry creek beds and sagebrush, what was a levee? Something mythic, like castle walls and towers? So, the word stuck in my consciousness; and as I grew older, I heard it in ballads and the blues.

Drove my Chevy to the levee, but the levee was dry . . .

As we walked along the levee holding hands . . .

If it keeps on rainin', levee's goin' to break
If it keeps on rainin', levee's goin' to break
When the levee breaks, I'll have no place to stay.

The lanterns on the levee, shine for you.

I've walked miles of Mississippi River levees, in the north and in the south. Levees contain the river, and they also retain the stories—stories of love, stories of laughter, stories of hard work, stories of enslavement and the walls of segregation. There are stories of levees breaking, and of levees blown up. Stories from the levees are the stories of life, intensified.

Thirty years ago, at the lower end of the Mississippi, about twenty miles south of Baton Rouge, Kathe Hambrick had a vision, standing on the levee. She recalls the day clearly: "As I turned my back to the mighty river and looked across the River Road, I saw the Tezcuco Plantation yard scattered with live oak trees and the fence lined with rows of sugarcane." And then she saw more. "I could see African people standing under the big oak trees and in the cane fields," she says. "It seems the ancestors were trying to tell me something."

That vision from the levee led Kathe Hambrick to build a museum, the River Road African American Museum, dedicated to stories of African Americans in the region. When the Tezcuco plantation house burned down a few years later, Hambrick relocated the museum in nearby Donaldsonville. There, the Mississippi River is an industrial channel, confined by the levees.

Here, there is no museum to honor the ancestors of Kaposia. But visions are still possible here. The levee along Kaposia Landing, quite literally, holds the strata of its stories. I look across the river to the east bank, and imagine, behind the oaks and cottonwoods, the people of Kaposia—Little Crow's village of Mdewakanton Dakota, near the marshy lake called Pig's Eye—who were forced out in 1837. They crossed the river and for a while, they lived here, along the west bank. Then the US-Dakota War broke out and drove them farther west. And when that war had ended, hundreds were confined in the concentration camp below the walls of Fort Snelling.

One day, early in May of 1863, the *Northerner*, a steamboat, passed by the empty fields of Kaposia on its way upriver to Fort Snelling. The *Northerner* had been ordered by the US government to remove the Dakota away from Fort Snelling. In tow, behind the *Northerner*, was a raft of refugees—African Americans from Missouri, fleeing slavery. The Emancipation

Proclamation, announced just a few months earlier by Abraham Lincoln, did not apply to the slaves of Missouri. So, a group of African Americans—seventy-some women and men, led by the Reverend Robert Hickman, set out on a raft, poling their way up the Mississippi River. Not quite knowing where they were headed, they called themselves *pilgrims*. As they struggled against the current, the *Northerner* came upon them and towed their raft north to Minnesota.

The captain of the *Northerner* intended to drop the raft of "pilgrims" at the city of Saint Paul. But when they reached the landing of Saint Paul's Lowertown, a mob of Irish workers gathered on the levee and prevented that from happening. So, the *Northerner* towed them on to Fort Snelling.

What happened at Fort Snelling is truly astounding—"one of those rare moments in history," writes William D. Green, "that summed up how the United States in the nineteenth century looked upon its two principal peoples of color." As the African Americans stepped off their raft, hundreds of Dakota were herded onto the *Northerner* to be taken away. The very same boat—rescuing one group of refugees and deporting another!

Reverend Hickman's pilgrims would go on to establish the Pilgrim Baptist Church. It remains a vital congregation in Saint Paul today, but the descendants of those pilgrims still suffer the ongoing racism and violence that has intensified this year. The stories keep on flowing.

In that same year of 1863, Jane Muckle was born in Belfast. When she was eighteen, she left Ireland and came to Minnesota, where she married Robert Robinson. They settled on the bluff in what would become South Saint Paul. Jane's story is renowned in the lore of Kaposia Landing.

For thirty-six years, Jane Muckle Robinson was the devoted post-light keeper of this stretch of the Mississippi River. Each evening, she rowed her wooden rowboat from Kaposia to Saint Paul to light four lanterns, placed strategically at the river's edge. And every morning, she rowed out again to extinguish the lights.

I visit Jane's grave, a mile back from the Mississippi, in the Oak Hill Cemetery. "Mother—Jane Robinson, 1863–1925." Other Robinsons are resting nearby. All around are gravestones bearing Irish and German and Scandinavian names. Farther up the hill stand the engraved stones of later immigrants—Polish, Serb, Croatian, and Romanian. From Jane's grave, you can look across the streets of central South Saint Paul; but the river itself remains unseen. Far to the east, the bluffs push up against the horizon.

I think of the bones of Jane Robinson, lying in the soil beneath me. I think on her life, of her thirty-six years on the Mississippi River, rowing, rowing, three or four miles each way on the river, morning and evening, a dozen or more miles a day. I imagine her strength, her stamina, pulling against wind and the current. The descending dark, the splash of the oars, the lapping of waves. Stepping into and out of the boat, kerosene can in hand, filling the lantern, trimming the wick, securing each light to its post. *Let the lower lights be burning, send a gleam across the wave.* What marvelous devotion—a life tending lanterns, making safe passage for nighttime travelers, all of whom have long since passed. Legendary folk singer Charlie Maguire celebrated Jane's story in "Light the River."

> Rowing on the water, spring-flood to fall
> > Four lights showing
> > whether clear or blowing

From Dayton Bluff to South Saint Paul
    Rowing on the water
    River woman Jane.

A river of time flows through Kaposia Landing, and the field
is its floodplain, protected now by a levee and built on the debris
of giant slaughterhouses. Green grass now grows over the past
century's rubble, and the wind blows steadily. I bring my grandson here to fly kites. Pamela and I pack a picnic. We run our
dogs in the dog park, or walk on the levee, holding hands.

When Jane began tending the lower lights along this shore,
long trains of cattle were beginning to arrive from Montana. In
the decades that followed, millions of animals would be butch-
ered and rendered. Blood flowed with the river. Workers, from
all across eastern Europe, came here to be packers and process-
ers of animal flesh. The town grew and prospered. Then, in the
fullness of time, it ended. The houses of Armour and Swift were
demolished, and the demolition debris spread over the floodplain, creating a landfill—Kaposia Landing. In time, the stench
of the stockyards also faded away.

It's spring, and the wind blows gently across the green fields.
I sit on a bench by the river, watching two towboats rearranging
barges. Pamela and I make our home not far from here, so we
come often to Kaposia Landing. In the stillness of this field, I
think about time and on all I have experienced and learned from
the river. I consider the voice of the gorge, the beauty of the
bluffs, the great bend in the river, and its many confluences.

What I find here is what I have yearned for throughout my
long journey—an experience of sanctuary. This plain, unadorned
field, bounded by river and railroad, open to the wings of eagles

and light planes alike, provides ample room to think about being in time. My illusions have no traction here. And neither has disillusion any grip on me. This stretch of the river is not like any I have known, and yet is the completion of all I have known.

Across the river, just up from Pig's Eye Lake, the city's wastewater gets discharged into the river—185 million gallons every day. This river that I contemplate is a river that flows through us—it's the water that we drink and the water that we flush. I've toured both water and wastewater treatment plants—stood in disoriented wonder in the dark, circular clarifying room of the Saint Paul Regional Water Services. Water from the Mississippi River is conveyed straight across the metro area through miles of enormous conduits, then brought down through a chain of lakes, to be purified for drinking. And once that purified water makes its way through us, and through our toilets and our showers, and has washed our clothes and washed our cars, it is sent on to the Metropolitan Wastewater Treatment Plant. Here, all that the river now carries—the dirt and feces, the toxins and the toilet paper, the plastics and the elusive pharmaceuticals—are filtered and treated. And when the water rejoins the Mississippi River current, it is cleaner than when it was withdrawn.

I joined a touring group of chemists, led by the affable plant manager, Dave Gardner. He likens wastewater treatment to the process of making beer and freely expresses joy in the details of his work. As the tour wrapped up, he recited his "Ode to Wastewater," concluding with a grin, "We're the unsung heroes of the sewer, the guardians of the river."

Jane Muckle Robinson was a river guardian in her time, keeping her four lanterns lit, all the while the sacred land was being desecrated. Now, I meet river guardians everywhere, like ministering angels: the Minnesota Water Stewards planting rain gardens to catch runoff, landscaping for clean water. Friends of the Mississippi River caring for the beauty and health of the gorge, and Friends of Pool 2, keeping watch on the river from Saint Paul to Hastings. The Lower Mississippi River Watershed Management Organization, monitoring water quality and levels of the lakes. There are other monitors, too, of chloride and pesticides, and ubiquitous microplastics. There are monitors of sediment—of sand, clay, and silt. There are those who trace chemicals that pass through our food chains—the persistent organic pollutants, tenacious PFCs and PCBs and PBDEs. These guardians are the river's acolytes, keepers of the lower lights.

In Kaposia Landing, a local baseball game is getting underway. A few people are walking over the fields and along the levee. Several bicyclists cross the railroad overpass from Simon's Ravine Trailhead. The towboats have departed; the barges remain moored. Across the river, an eagle circles and alights in the top of a cottonwood, beside its mate. A soft wind from the south ripples the water and bends the grasses. A stalk of Dame's Rocket nods, its lavender petals are brilliant and trembling. On the far side, a long, slow-moving train of black tank cars stops suddenly, sending a sound like the roll of thunder down the entire length of Kaposia Landing. Nothing is distracting. I breathe deeply. I am here. Now. In this time. In this place.

REFERENCES

PROLOGUE: CONSIDER THE RIVER

Bennett, Jane. *The Enchantment of Modern Life: Attachments, Crossings, and Ethics.* Princeton, NJ: Princeton University Press, 2016.

Lewis, C. S. *Surprised by Joy: The Shape of My Early Life.* New York: Harcourt Brace, 1995, 69.

Momaday, N. Scott. *The Man Made of Words.* New York: St. Martin's Griffin, 1997.

Moore, Thomas. *The Re-Enchantment of Everyday Life.* New York: HarperCollins, 1996.

Smith, Thomas Ruys. *River of Dreams: Imagining the Mississippi before Mark Twain.* Baton Rouge: Louisiana State University Press, 2007.

Wright, Richard. *Black boy, a record of childhood and youth.* New York: Harper & Bros., 1945.

BRIDGE: LOOKING INTO THE GORGE

Anfinson, John O. "The Secret History of the Mississippi's Earliest Locks and Dams." *Minnesota History* 54 (Summer 1995): 254–267.

Arey, Richard Fred. *Waterfalls of the Mississippi: The Story of Eight Waterfalls Found in Saint Paul & Minneapolis.* Wood engravings by Gaylord Schanilec. Saint Paul: Minnesota Outdoors Press, 1998.

Doell, C. D. "Minnehaha Falls and Longfellow's 'Hiawatha.'" *Minnesota History,* September 1927.

Donahue, Brian. "'Dammed at Both Ends and Cursed in the Middle:' The 'Flowage' of the Concord River Meadows, 1798–1862." *Environmental Review* 13 (Autumn/Winter 1989): 46–67.

Holmes, Hilary. "Bridal Veil Falls." *Open Rivers: Rethinking the Mississippi*, no. 5 (2017). http://editions.lib.umn.edu/openrivers/article/bridal-veil-falls/.

Leaf, Sue. *Minnesota's Geologist: the Life of Newton Horace Winchell.* Minneapolis: University of Minnesota Press, 2020.

Lenhart, Christian. "Restoration of the Mississippi River Gorge: Issues and Research Needs." *Ecological Restoration* 30, no. 3 (September 2012): 218–227.

Marcotty, Josephine. "Alarm Raised About 3 Area Rivers: Group Cites Dam Removals as Chance to restore Rivers to Wild." *Minneapolis Star Tribune,* April 10, 2018.

Monkhouse, Christopher. "Henry Wadsworth Longfellow and the Mississippi River." In *Currents of Change: Art and Life Along the Mississippi River, 1850–1869,* edited by Jason Busch, Christopher Monkhouse, and Janet Whitmore. Minneapolis: University of Minnesota Press, 2004.

Schussler, Edith May. *Doctors, Dynamite, and Dogs.* Caldwell, ID: Caxton Printers, 1956.

Schussler, Otto F. *Riverside Reveries.* Minneapolis: s.n. 1928.

Severson, Megan. "Corps Opens a Floodgate of Debate Over Twin Cities Locks & Dams." *Big River* (September/October 2018): 20–23.

Trenerry, Walter N. "The Case of the Convenient Cliff." In *Murder in Minnesota: A Collection of True Cases.* Saint Paul: Minnesota Historical Society, 1962.

Tuan, Yi-Fu. *Space and Place: The Perspective of Experience.* Minneapolis: University of Minnesota Press, 1977.

"Woman Loses Life in Effort to Rescue Dog." *Minneapolis Sunday Tribune* (November 29, 1914), 1. http://newspapers2.mnhs.org/jsp/viewer.jsp?doc_id=mnhi0005%2F1DFC5G5B%2F14112901&init_width=600&recoffset=300&collection_filter=All&collection_name=28c436b4-f574-4314-9c39-86d7a7d4924c&sort_col=Title&CurSearchNum=-1&recOffset=300.

Wright, H. E. Jr. *Geologic History of Minnesota Rivers.* St. Paul: University of Minnesota, 1990.

CONFLUENCE: WHERE WATERS COME TOGETHER

Ahlgren, Dorothy Eaton, and Mary Cotter Beeler. *A History of Prescott, Wisconsin: A River City and Farming Community on the St. Croix and Mississippi.* Saint Paul: Minnesota Historical Society, 1996.

Aron, Stephen. *American Confluence: The Missouri Frontier from Borderland to Border State.* Bloomington: Indiana University Press, 2006.

Carroll, Jane Lamm. "Naginowenah, Lucy Prescott, and the Wizard of Cereal Foods: Cultural Identity Across Three Generations of an Anglo-Dakota Family." *Minnesota History* 63 (Summer 2012): 58–68.

Carroll, Peter Neil. *Riverborne: A Mississippi Requiem.* Higganum, CT: Higganum Hill Books, 2007.

Chopin, Kate. "Her Letters." *Vogue,* April 11/18, 1895.

Cram, Thomas J. *Basin of the Mississippi and Its Natural Business Site at the Confluence of the Ohio and Mississippi Rivers, Briefly Considered.* New York: Narine & Co., 1851.

DeCarlo, Peter. *Fort Snelling at Bdote: A Brief History.* Saint Paul: Minnesota Historical Society Press, 2016.

Duncan, Dayton. *Scenes of Visionary Enchantment: Reflections on Lewis and Clark.* Lincoln: University of Nebraska Press, 2004.

Eliot, T. S. Introduction to *The Adventures of Huckleberry Finn* by Mark Twain. London: Cresset Press, 1950.

Eliot, T. S. "Letter to Marquis Childs." Quoted in *St. Louis Post Dispatch,* October 15, 1930.

Lansden, John M. *A History of the City of Cairo, Illinois.* Carbondale: Southern Illinois University Press, 1976.

Marquette, Jacques. *The Mississippi Voyage of Jolliet and Marquette, 1673.* Wisconsin Historical Society, Digital Library and Archives. https://content.wisconsinhistory.org/digital/collection/aj/id/3097.

Morris, Larry E. *The Fate of the Corps: What Became of the Lewis and Clark Explorers After the Expedition.* New Haven, CT: Yale University Press, 2004.

Muir, John. *The Story of My Boyhood and Youth.* Boston: Houghton Mifflin, 1913. https://www.gutenberg.org/ebooks/18359.

Ordway, John. "Letter of John Ordway of Lewis and Clark Expedition to His Parents." *Quarterly of the Oregon Historical Society* 23 (September 1, 1922): 268–269. The original resides in the Oregon Historical Society. This material is made available, free to anyone, through Early Journal Content on JSTOR. https://ia801909.us.archive.org/34/items/jstor-20610217/20610217.pdf.

Passer, Oleg, dir. *Camp River Dubois.* Saint Louis, MO: Solstice Productions, 2006. https://www.dailymotion.com/video/x1zq9oe.

Ping, Wang. "A Fig in Cairo." In *Life of Miracles Along the Yangtze and Mississippi.* Athens: University of Georgia Press, 2018.

Powers, Ron. *Far from Home: Life and Loss in Two American Towns.* New York: Random House, 1991.

Prescott, Philander. *The Recollections of Philander Prescott: Frontiersman of the Old Northwest, 1819–1862.* Edited by Donald Dean Parker. Lincoln: University of Nebraska Press, 1966.

Rice, Stephen P., André G. Roy, and Bruce L. Rhoads. *River Confluences, Tributaries and the Fluvial Network.* Hoboken, NJ: John Wiley & Sons, 2008.

Stevens, John H. *Personal Recollections of Minnesota and its People: Early History of Minneapolis.* Minneapolis: Tribune Job Ptg. Co., 1890.

Waters, Thomas F. *The Streams and Rivers of Minnesota.* Minneapolis: University of Minnesota Press, 1977.

Wohl, Ellen. "The Mississippi: Once and Future River." In *A World of Rivers: Environmental Change on Ten of the World's Great Rivers.* Chicago: University of Chicago Press, 2010.

Yeoman, Barry. "Life on the Mississippi, Now." *OnEarth*, January 5, 2016. https://www.nrdc.org/onearth/life-mississippi-now.

BEND: A PLACE OF AWFUL QUIET

Avery, Valeen Tippetts. *From Mission to Madness: Last Son of the Mormon Prophet.* Urbana: University of Illinois Press, 1998.

Beam, Alex. *American Crucifixion: The Murder of Joseph Smith and the Fate of the Mormon Church.* New York: Public Affairs, 2014.

Bishop, M. Guy. "'What Has Become of Our Fathers?' Baptism for the Dead at Nauvoo." *Dialogue: A Journal of Mormon Thought* 23 (Summer 1990): 85–97.

Black, Susan E. "Nauvoo Neighbor: The Latter-day Experience at the Mississippi River, 1843–45." *BYU Studies* 51 (2012):141+.

Bray, Robert T. "Times and Seasons: An Archaeological Perspective on Early Latter Day Saints Printing." *Historical Archaeology* 13 (1979): 53–119.

Brown, Samuel Morris. *In Heaven as It Is on Earth: Joseph Smith and the Early Mormon Conquest of Death.* Oxford, UK: Oxford University Press, 2012.

Chambers, Julius. *The Mississippi River and its Wonderful Valley: Twenty-Seven Hundred and Seventy-Five Miles from Source to Sea.* New York: Putnam's, 1910.

Chambers, Julius. "Walks and Talks." *Brooklyn Daily Eagle,* June 7, 1907, 30.

Christensen, Rex Leroy. *The Life and Contributions of Captain Dan Jones.* Utah State University, 1977.

Compier, Don H. "The Faith of Emma Smith." *John Whitmer Historical Association Journal* 6 (1986): 64–72.

Cope, Rachel. "A Sacred Space for Women: Hymnody in Emma Hale Smith's Theology." *Journal of Religious History* 42 (June 2018): 242–264.

Enders, Donald L. "The Steamboat *Maid of Iowa:* Mormon Mistress of the Mississippi." *BYU Studies* 19, no. 3 (1979).

Flanders, Robert Bruce. *Nauvoo: Kingdom on the Mississippi.* Urbana: University of Illinois Press, 1965.

Grow, Matthew L. *Liberty to the Downtrodden: Thomas L. Kane, Romantic Reformer.* Princeton, NJ: Yale University Press, 2009.

Haven, Charlotte. "A Girl's Letters from Nauvoo." *Overland Monthly* 16 (December 1890): 616–638; "A Girl's Letters from Nauvoo II." *Overland Monthly* 17 (February 1891):145–51. http://www.olivercowdery.com/smithhome/1880s-1890s/havn1890.htm#Charl.

Hinckley, Gordon B. "Nauvoo—Sunrise and Sunset on the Mississippi." *BYU Studies* 32 (Winter/Spring 1992): 19–22.

Kane, Thomas L. *The Mormons: A Discourse Delivered before the Historical Society of Pennsylvania, March 26, 1850.* Philadelphia: King & Baird, 1850.

Krakauer, Jon. *Under the Banner of Heaven: A Story of Violent Faith.* New York: Doubleday, 2003.

Laquer, Thomas. *The Work of the Dead: A Cultural History of Mortal Remains.* Princeton, NJ: Princeton University Press, 2015.

Meyers, Mary Ann. "Gates Ajar: Death in Mormon Thought and Practice." In *Death in America,* edited by David E. Stannard. Philadelphia: University of Pennsylvania Press (1976), 112–133.

Newell, Linda King, and Valeen Tippets Avery. *Mormon Enigma: Emma Hale Smith,* 2nd ed. Urbana: University of Illinois Press, 1994.

Ostling, Richard N., and Joan K. Ostling. *Mormon America: The Power and the Promise.* New York: HarperOne, 2007.

Perry, Seth. "Go Down into Jordan: No, Mississippi. Mormon Nauvoo and the Rhetoric of Landscape." In *Gods of the Mississippi,* edited by Michael Pasquier. Bloomington, Indiana University Press (2013), 95–112.

Pykles, Benjamin C. *Excavating Nauvoo: The Mormons and the Rise of Historical Archaeology in America.* Lincoln: University of Nebraska Press, 2010.

Quinn, D. Michael. "The Practice of Rebaptism at Nauvoo." *BYU Studies* 18, no. 2 (Winter 1978): 226–232.

Romig, Ronald, ed. *Emma's Nauvoo,* 2nd ed. Independence, MO: John Whitmer Books, 2007.

Rowley, Dennis. "Nauvoo: A River Town." *BYU Studies* 18, no. 2 (Winter 1978): 255+.

Smith, Joseph. "Sermon Delivered April 7, 1844 ('King Follet Sermon')." *American Sermons: The Pilgrims to Martin Luther King, Jr.* New York: Library of America, 1999.

Snow, Eliza R. *The Complete Poetry.* Edited by Jill Mulvay Derr and Karen Lynn Davidson. Provo, UT: Brigham Young University Press, 2009.

Stegner, Wallace. *The Gathering of Zion: The Story of the Mormon Trail.* New York: McGraw Hill, 1964.

Woodruff, Wilford. "Discourse Delivered by President Wilford Woodruff at the General Conference, in the Tabernacle, Salt Lake City, Monday Morning, April 6, 1891." *Deseret Weekly* 42, no. 18 (25 April 1891): 553-4. https://contentdm.lib.byu.edu/digital/collection/desnews4/id/18928/rec/1

BLUFFS: STALKING THE SACRED

Flanagan, John T. "Thoreau in Minnesota." *Minnesota History* 16 (March 1935): 35–46.

Harding, Walter. "Thoreau and Mann on the Minnesota River, June, 1861." *Minnesota History* 37 (June 1961).

Harding, Walter, ed. *Thoreau's Minnesota Journey: Two Documents.* Geneseo, NY: Thoreau Society, 1962.

Klauza, Matthew D. "Mark Twain, Homesickness, and Hannibal." *Mark Twain Journal,* 48 (Spring/Fall 2010): 49–103.

Meinig, D. W. "The Beholding Eye: Ten Versions of the Same Scene." In *The Interpretation of Ordinary Landscapes: Geographical Essays,* edited by D. W. Meinig and John Brinckerhoff Jackson. New York: Oxford University Press, 1979.

Momaday, N. Scott. *The Man Made of Words.* New York: St. Martin's Griffin, 1997.

Moore, Thomas. *The Re-Enchantment of Everyday Life.* New York: HarperCollins, 1996.

Palmer, Parker. *The Active Life: Wisdom for Work, Creativity, and Caring.* New York: HarperCollins, 1990.

Parker, Hershel. *Herman Melville: A Biography, Vol I, 1819–1851.* Baltimore: Johns Hopkins (1996), 177.

Pasquier, Michael, ed. *Gods of the Mississippi.* Bloomington: Indiana University Press, 2013.

Philippon, Daniel. "Thoreau's Notes on the Journey West: Nature Writing or Environmental History?" *American Transcendental Quarterly* 18, no. 2 (June 2004): 105.

Powers, Ron. *Mark Twain: A Life.* New York: Free Press, 2005.

Rubenstein, Sarah Paskins. *Minnesota History Along the Highways: A Guide to Historic Markers and Sites.* Minnesota Historical Society Press, 2003.

Sanborn, Franklin B., ed. *The First and Last Journeys of Thoreau: Lately Discovered Among His Unpublished Journals and Manuscripts,* vol. 2. Boston: Bibliophile Society, 1905.

Sealts, Merton M., Jr. "The Ghost of Major Melvill." *New England Quarterly* 30 (September 1957): 291–306.

Smith, Corinne Hosfeld. *Westward I Go Free: Tracing Thoreau's Last Journey.* Winnipeg, Manitoba: Green Frigate Books, 2012.

Tanselle, G. Thomas. "Herman Melville's Visit to Galena." *Journal of Illinois State Historical Society* 53, no. 4 (Winter 1960): 376–388.

Thoreau, Henry David. *Familiar Letters of Henry David Thoreau.* Edited by F. B. Sanborn. Boston: Houghton Mifflin, 1894.

Twain, Mark. *Life on the Mississippi.* Boston: James R. Osgood, 1883.

Twain, Mark. *The Adventures of Huckleberry Finn.* New York: Charles L. Webster, 1885.

Twain, Mark. *The Adventures of Tom Sawyer.* Hartford: American Publishing Co., 1884.

FIELD: KAPOSIA LANDING

Carley, Kenneth. *The Dakota War of 1862.* Saint Paul: Minnesota Historical Society Press, 1976.

Durant, Thomas J. *Our Roots Run Deep: A History of the River Road African American Museum.* Donning Company Publishers, 2002.

Glewwe, Lois A. *South St. Paul: A Brief History.* Charleston, SC: History Press, 2015.

Green, William D. *The Children of Lincoln: White Paternalism and the Limits of Black Opportunity in Minnesota, 1860–1876.* Minneapolis: University of Minnesota Press, 2018.

ABOUT THE AUTHOR
AND THE ILLUSTRATOR

Thomas Becknell grew up on the plains and prairies of Wyoming and Nebraska. He received his PhD from the University of Iowa and taught literature and writing in Saint Paul, Minnesota, for thirty-five years. His early love of stories, creeks, and streams led to a later fascination with the Mississippi River, and to the writing of this book. You can contact him for speaking engagements, book club discussions, and interviews at www.thomasbecknell.com.

Kari Vick's childhood home was perched on the edge of a bluff above the Mississippi River in Red Wing, Minnesota. Bright lights of passing barges lit up her bedroom walls at night as lonely trains whistled their way along the river valley far below. She kayaked the slinky river bottoms with her husband, Jim, a kindred river rat. They now live and paddle along the north shore of Lake Superior in Lutsen, Minnesota. This is the ninth book she has illustrated. You can find more of her work at www.karivick.com.